THE SHAMAN'S PATH FOR BEGINNERS

CLEAR AND EASY GUIDANCE, BASIC INTERPRETATION TECHNIQUES, AND REAL-LIFE APPLICATIONS FOR YOUR JOURNEY INTO HOLISTIC HEALTH

IGGY GARCIA

CONTENTS

INTRODUCTION

Years ago, while hiking Huyna Picchu, I stood on a ridge, gazing at the vast expanse below. The air was thin, and the silence was profound. Suddenly, a condor swooped down, its shadow passing over me. At that moment, I felt a connection to something much more significant than myself. This experience, both humbling and exhilarating, was a powerful catalyst that led me to the world of shamanism, a journey I am excited to share with you.

This book, "The Shaman's Path for Beginners: Clear and Easy Guidance, Basic Interpretation Techniques, and Real-life Applications for Your Journey into Holistic Health," aims to guide you on a similar journey. My goal is to introduce you to the transformative power of shamanic practices. These ancient techniques can be adapted to fit our modern lives, offering tools for personal growth and self-healing.

So, what is shamanism? Shamanism is a spiritual practice that involves connecting with nature and the spirit world to gain insights and healing. It is a path that has been walked by many cultures around the globe for thousands of years. Shamans act as intermediaries between the physical and spiritual realms, using rituals, meditations, and energy to bring balance and harmony.

Allow me to introduce myself. My name is Ignacio, but you can call me Iggy. I'm a native of Peru and have been immersed in the sacred ways of Peruvian Shamanism for many years. I hold titles such as Peruvian Shaman, Medicine Man, Minister, Chief, and Elder. My journey has led me to become a spiritual leader in my community in Columbus, Ohio.

My path has been anything but ordinary. I've walked the red road with The Condor Eagle Society and The Nemenhah Indigenous Traditional Organization. I've also been involved in various holistic and metaphysical practices. For over two decades, I've hosted a weekly internet podcast and radio show, sharing insights and stories from my journey. My heart belongs to The Condor Eagle Society in Columbus, Ohio, where I continue to practice and teach the sacred ways.

This book aims to uncover the rich tapestry of shamanic practices that have shaped human history and imagination. You will learn to tap into your innate ability to heal physically, emotionally, and spiritually through guided meditations, energy work, and intuitive practices. Always remember, IT'S GOOD TO BE HERE!

In today's fast-paced world, shamanism offers a way to reconnect with nature and ourselves. It provides a framework for understanding our place in the universe and offers tools for personal transformation. Shamanic practices can guide you whether you seek to heal old wounds, gain clarity, or find peace.

Customer research strongly suggests that many beginners feel overwhelmed when they first approach shamanism. They worry about not having enough experience or not knowing where to start. This book is designed with you in mind. It breaks down complex concepts into easy-to-understand steps. You don't need prior knowledge to benefit from the practices outlined here.

I promise that by the end of this book, you will have a solid foundation in shamanic practices. You will learn how to conduct shamanic journeys, perform rituals, and use healing techniques. More importantly, you will gain the confidence to incorporate these practices into your daily life.

So, take a deep breath and relax. You're about to embark on a journey that will transform you in ways you never imagined. Each chapter will guide you through different aspects of shamanism, from understanding its history to practicing its rituals.

I encourage you to keep an open mind and a willing heart. The path of the shaman is one of discovery and growth. It's a journey that requires patience, but the rewards are profound. You will connect with your true self and the world around you in ancient and profoundly modern ways.

Welcome to the journey. Let's begin.

CHAPTER 1
FOUNDATIONS OF SHAMANISM

Have you ever chatted with a tree? I did once, and it wasn't just the altitude talking. Perched on a rock in the Amazon rainforest, I was deep in meditation when an ancient tree seemed to whisper ancient secrets. As absurd as it sounds, this experience opened my eyes to the shamanic worldview, where everything is alive, interconnected, and brimming with spirit. This chapter lays the groundwork for understanding these profound beliefs, setting the stage for your exploration into shamanism.

1.1 UNDERSTANDING THE SHAMANIC WORLDVIEW

The interconnected nature of reality in shamanic belief is a concept that might initially seem foreign, yet it is incredibly intuitive. Shamanism posits that everything in the universe is interconnected, forming a complex web of life. This isn't just poetic musings; it's a core shamanic tenet. Picture a spider's web glistening with morning dew – every strand is crucial, and the vibration of one affects the entire structure. In the shamanic worldview, every being, whether human, animal, plant, or stone, has a spirit and contributes to this intricate web.

Consider the ways nature exemplifies this interconnectedness. The symbiotic relationship between bees and flowers, the way trees communicate through mycorrhizal networks, and even how a walk in the park can lift your mood are all manifestations of the web of life. Shamanism teaches that this web isn't just ecological but spiritual. Every being has a spiritual essence, a unique energy contributing to the whole. This belief fosters a deep respect for all life forms and a sense of responsibility for maintaining balance and harmony within the web.

Shamanic cosmology delineates the universe into three worlds: the Upper World, the Middle World, and the Lower World. These realms are not merely physical spaces but energetic dimensions that shamans navigate to gain wisdom and healing. The Upper World is a realm of higher spiritual beings and elevated conscious-ness. Imagine it as a celestial library where the most enlightened spirits reside, offering guidance and wisdom. The Middle World, our everyday reality, is also teeming with spirits – think of it as the bustling marketplace of the soul, where both ordinary and extraordinary beings interact. Lastly, the Lower World is a treasure trove of ancient wisdom and healing energies, often inhabited by power animals and ancestral spirits. It's like diving into the ocean's depths, where hidden treasures and profound insights await.

The shaman's role as a mediator or mentor is to be balanced and listen to what is spoken (the art of listening) to help bring harmony. Shamans act as bridges between these worlds, facili-tating communication and healing and reminding us that all healing is self-healing. They don't just chat with spirits for fun (though who wouldn't want to?). They perform vital functions, mediating between humans and the spiritual realm to bring back wisdom, healing, and guidance. Shamans serve their communi-ties by performing healing ceremonies, guiding individuals through personal crises, and maintaining the spiritual well-being of the group. Think of them as spiritual diplomats, negotiating the delicate balance between the seen and unseen worlds.

Nature holds a place of paramount importance in shamanic prac-tice. It's not just the backdrop for rituals; it's a teacher, healer, and source of wisdom. Shamans believe that nature's rhythms and cycles offer profound lessons. The changing seasons, the phases of the moon, the migration patterns of animals – all these natural phenomena are reflections of deeper spiritual truths. Spending time in nature, meditating by a river, or observing the sky can help you connect more deeply with these natural cycles. You tap into its inherent wisdom and healing power by aligning yourself with nature.

To truly grasp the shamanic worldview, one must embrace the idea that the world is alive and buzzing with spiritual energy. This perspective invites you to see the world with new eyes, to recognize the spirit in all things, and to engage with the universe as a living, breathing entity. Through this lens, every interaction and moment becomes an opportunity for spiritual connection and growth.

So, take a moment to breathe deeply and feel the world around you. The tree outside your window, the bird singing its morning song, and even the stone beneath your feet are part of the same vibrant, interconnected web of life. As you continue this book, you'll discover how to engage with this web meaningfully, unlocking the wisdom and healing it offers.

1.2 THE ROLE OF THE SHAMAN IN ANCIENT CULTURES

Shamanism, one of the oldest spiritual practices, traces its origins back to hunter-gatherer societies that roamed the Earth millennia ago. Imagine ancient tribes huddled around fires, seeking guidance and healing from those uniquely attuned to the spiritual realms – the shamans. These individuals were the first to walk the path, connecting with the unseen and bringing back wisdom to their communities. Shamanic practices have evolved, yet they have retained their core principles. Shamanic traditions have persisted from Siberia's icy tundras to the Amazon's dense rainforests, with each culture adding a unique flavor to the practice.

In indigenous cultures, shamans served as the backbone of their communities. They were the healers, the spiritual leaders, and the mediators who bridged the gap between the physical and spiritual worlds. When someone fell ill, the shaman diagnosed the ailment, often attributing it to spiritual imbalances or evil spirits. Through rituals, chants, and the use of sacred tools, they worked to restore harmony and health. But healing wasn't their only role. Shamans led community rituals that marked the changing seasons, celebrated harvests, and honored the spirits of the land. They offered spiritual guidance, interpreted dreams and omens, and provided counsel during times of crisis. In essence, shamans were the glue that held the spiritual fabric of their communities together.

Shamanic rituals and ceremonies were diverse and profound, each serving a specific purpose. Healing ceremonies were the most common, where the shaman would enter a trance state, often induced by rhythmic drumming or the ingestion of sacred plants. In this altered state, they would journey to the spirit world, seeking the assistance of spirit guides and power animals to diagnose and cure ailments. Seasonal rituals marked the passage of time, ensuring the community stayed harmonized with nature's cycles. These rituals could involve offerings to the spirits, dances, drum circles, and communal feasts. Rites of passage were equally important, guiding individuals through significant life transitions such as birth, puberty, marriage, and death. Each ceremony was deeply spiritual, reinforcing the community's connection to the spiritual world.

Becoming a shaman wasn't a personal choice but a spiritual calling. Selection often began with dreams, visions, or unusual experiences indicating that the spirits had chosen an individual. This calling was only sometimes welcomed, as the path of a shaman was fraught with challenges (in my case, I wanted to be something other than a shaman). Once chosen, the apprentice would undergo rigorous training and initiation rites. This training could last many years and involved learning medicinal plants, mastering various rituals, and developing the ability to enter trance states. The initiation rites were often grueling, involving periods of isolation, fasting, and intense spiritual trials. These experiences were designed to break down the apprentice's ego, allowing them to be reborn as a conduit for spiritual power.

In many cultures, the initiation involved symbolic death and rebirth. The apprentice might undergo a vision quest, spending days alone in the wilderness, fasting and seeking visions. They would return with newfound wisdom and a deeper connection to the spirit world. The community would then formally recognize their transformation through a public ceremony, marking their transition from apprentice to shaman. This process ensured that only those indeed called and prepared could take on the role of a shaman.

The role of the shaman in ancient cultures was multifaceted and deeply integrated into daily life. They were healers, spiritual leaders, and keepers of wisdom. Their practices and rituals benefitted individuals and the entire community, ensuring everyone remained in harmony with the spiritual and natural worlds. Through their unique connection to the spirits, shamans provided guidance, healing, and wisdom, helping their communities navigate the complexities of life.

1.3 SPIRIT GUIDES AND POWER ANIMALS: AN OVERVIEW

Imagine traversing a dense, nocturnal forest, with only the faint moonlight filtering through the trees and the faltering beam of your flashlight for guidance. Suddenly, a fox appears, guiding you with swift, graceful movements. This is no ordinary encounter; the fox is a powerful animal, a spiritual ally offering protection and insight. In shamanism, spirit guides and power animals are essential, serving as mentors, protectors, and sources of strength and enlightenment. Spirit guides can manifest as ancestors, divine figures, or mystical beings, imparting wisdom and direction, while power animals embody specific qualities and abilities, providing protection and guidance when needed. Connecting with these spiritual companions is a transformative and deeply personal journey. Find a serene spot through guided visualizations, close your eyes, and breathe deeply. Picture yourself in a tranquil natural environment, like a forest or meadow, and call forth your spirit guide or power animal. Trust in the visions that appear, even if they are products of your imagination. Another method to forge this connection is through shamanic journeys. With the help of rhythmic drumming or rattling, enter a trance-like state to journey into the spiritual realm, where you can meet and interact with your guides and animal spirits, seeking their guidance and wisdom. These practices enrich your spiritual path by deepening your bond with your spiritual allies.

Spirit guides and power animals play crucial roles in shamanic work. They provide insights and messages through visions, dreams, or intuitive feelings. During a healing session, a shaman may call upon a powerful animal to lend its strength and protection. For instance, a bear might offer its formidable power to help someone overcome fear, while an eagle could provide a higher perspective on a difficult situation. These spiritual allies also assist in energy healing, guiding the shaman to areas that need attention and helping to restore balance and harmony. Their presence is a reminder that we are never alone on our path.

I want to share a personal anecdote to show the impact of spirit guides and power animals. Several years ago, I was working with a client who struggled with anxiety and self-doubt. During a shamanic journey, a majestic lion appeared as her power animal. This lion exuded confidence and strength, qualities my client desperately needed. Over time, she began to embody these traits, finding the courage to pursue her dreams and stand up for herself. The transformation was remarkable, and it all started with that initial encounter with her power animal. Another practitioner I know often speaks of when a wise owl guided her through intense grief, offering comfort and clarity when she needed it most.

Connecting with your spirit guides and power animals is not a one-time event but an ongoing relationship. Regular communication, whether through meditation, journeying, or simply being mindful of their presence, strengthens this bond. You might notice signs and synchronicities in your daily life, such as recurring symbols or animals appearing in unexpected places. These are gentle reminders of your spiritual allies' presence and support. Keep a journal to document these experiences, as they can offer valuable insights and guidance over time.

Spirit guides and power animals are invaluable allies in shamanic practice, offering wisdom, protection, and healing. You tap into a wellspring of spiritual strength and insight by connecting with them. Whether seeking guidance through challenging times or deepening your spiritual practice, these spiritual allies support and guide you. Their presence enriches your journey, helping you navigate the complexities of life with greater ease and confidence.

1.4 THE SHAMANIC JOURNEY: EXPLORING NON-ORDINARY REALITIES

A shamanic journey is like taking a spiritual detour from the mundane to the magical. Imagine closing your eyes and, instead of seeing darkness, finding yourself in a lush forest or an ethereal realm where spirits and guides await. This isn't a flight of fancy but a purposeful exploration of non-ordinary realities. The purpose of these journeys can range from seeking healing, gaining guidance, or uncovering hidden wisdom. Shamans and those who practice these techniques travel to alternate dimensions of reality where the rules of physics bend and the boundaries of the mind expand.

Now, how does one even begin to undertake such a mystical voyage? It starts with preparing the mind and body. Find a quiet space where you won't be disturbed. Sit or lie comfortably, close your eyes, and take several deep breaths. This calms your mind and prepares you for the journey ahead. It's also essential to set a clear intention. Are you seeking healing? Guidance? Perhaps you're looking to connect with a spirit guide. Whatever it is, focus on this intention as you begin.

The next step is entering a trance state, which can be achieved through various techniques. One standard method is rhythmic drumming or rattling, which helps alter your consciousness. The drum's steady beat mimics the Earth's heartbeat, guiding you into deeper awareness. You might also use visualization techniques, imagining yourself descending a staircase or walking through a tunnel to reach the spiritual realm. Once you're in this altered state, allow the journey to unfold naturally, following your intuition.

The shamanic journey takes you through three primary realms: Here is the Inka Cosmology and the power animals' version of the Lower World (Ukhu Pacha) snake, the Middle World (Kay Pacha) puma, and the Upper World (Hanaq Pacha) condor. Each has its unique significance and offers different types of wisdom. The Lower World is a place of profound insight and healing energies. Here, you might encounter power animals, ancestral spirits, or other benevolent beings who offer their wisdom and guidance. Navigating this world can bring deep understanding and transformation.

The Upper World, on the other hand, is a realm of higher spiritual beings and elevated consciousness. It's like accessing a cosmic library where enlightened spirits reside, ready to share their knowledge. Seeking guidance in the Upper World can clarify your life's purpose or solve your challenges. The Middle World, while not a primary focus during shamanic journeys, is still significant. It mirrors our physical reality but includes all spiritual dimensions, making it a place where spirits from the Upper and Lower Worlds can interact.

Intention and safety are paramount when journeying to these realms. Setting a clear and respectful intention ensures that you enter the experience with purpose and focus. Always approach these journeys with a sense of reverence and humility, acknowledging the sacredness of the process. Safety measures are equally important. Before you begin, create protection around yourself by visualizing a favorite color, and create armor or a sphere around you. Then, pick a number 1-10. I call it the escape hatch that brings you back to the present moment and safe sound (remember, this is your journey. You are in control). Then, ground yourself by visualizing roots extending from your body into the Earth. This grounding keeps you anchored, ensuring you can return safely from your journey. Upon your return, take a moment to reorient yourself. Wiggle your fingers and toes, take deep breaths, and slowly open your eyes. If you want to know if you are back, do multiplication 5x5=25, and if you say 36, you are not grounded and need to work your way back slowly.

One practical step to enhance safety is to keep a journal nearby. After each journey, could you write down your experiences, insights, and any messages received? This not only helps you remember but also aids in integrating the wisdom gained into your daily life. Sharing your experiences with a trusted friend or mentor can provide additional perspectives and support.

In summary, a shamanic journey is a powerful tool for exploring non-ordinary realities, offering healing, guidance, and wisdom. By preparing your mind and body, setting clear intentions, and ensuring safety, you can confidently and respectfully navigate the realms of the Lower, Middle, and Upper Worlds. This practice opens doors to profound spiritual experiences, enriching your life in ways you might never have imagined. So, take a deep breath and let the journey begin.

1.5 ESSENTIAL TOOLS OF THE SHAMAN: DRUMS, RATTLES, AND FEATHERS

Have you ever thought a drum could be more than just an instrument? In shamanic practice, drums, rattles, and feathers hold profound significance. Let's start with the drum. To a shaman, the drum is a tool and a heartbeat connecting us to the Earth. Imagine a drumbeat's steady, rhythmic pulse echoing the Earth's rhythm. This repetitive sound helps shamans enter trance states, allowing them to travel to spiritual realms. The drumbeat becomes a bridge, guiding the shaman into deeper states of consciousness. It's akin to how a lullaby can soothe a baby to sleep; the drum's beat lulls the mind into a meditative state, opening doors to the spiritual world.

Rattles, on the other hand, are like your spiritual broom. They break up stagnant energy and clear the space, creating new, vibrant energy. Picture a room filled with dust and cobwebs. Just as you'd use a broom to clean it, the shaman uses the rattle to cleanse the energy field. The sound of the rattle disrupts negative or stuck energy, allowing it to disperse and be replaced with positive vibrations. This makes rattles invaluable in healing rituals that restore balance and harmony.

Feathers, simple yet elegant gifts from the sky, symbolize flight and spiritual messages. They are often used in rituals to call upon spirits or to send prayers to the heavens. Imagine the feather as a pen, writing your intentions and prayers into the air and carrying them to the spirit world. Holding a feather and feeling its lightness can also remind us of the importance of being light-hearted and open to spiritual guidance.

Using these tools effectively requires a bit of know-how. For drums, it's not just about banging away; there's a method to the madness. Different rhythms serve different purposes. A steady, monotonous beat helps you enter a trance state, while more complex rhythms can be used for specific rituals. When using a rattle, it's all about intention and movement. Shake the rattle around your body or the space you're cleansing, focusing on heavy or stuck areas. Feathers can be used in various ways, such as waving them to disperse smoke during a smudging ceremony or holding them while you meditate to invite spiritual insights.

Acquiring shamanic tools is a unique process. It's not like shopping for groceries. These tools should resonate with you on a deeper level. You might find a drum that seems to call out to you or a feather that catches your eye during a walk in the woods. Once you've found a tool that speaks to you, it's important to consecrate it. This can be done through rituals that involve cleansing the tool with sage smoke, dedicating it with a prayer, and setting an intention for its use. This process imbues the tool with your energy and aligns it with your spiritual practice.

I'd like to share a story to illustrate this. A friend, who is not a shamanic practitioner, once found an old, worn-out drum at a pawn shop. It looked ordinary, even shabby. But when she picked it up, she felt an instant connection. She took it home, cleaned it, and consecrated it in her special ceremony. That drum became one of her favorite powerful drums, often guiding her to profound spiritual insights in the drum circle and during her rituals. It's a reminder that the power of a tool lies not in its appearance but in the connection and intention behind it.

Different cultures have their unique practices and tools. In some Native American traditions, eagle feathers are considered especially sacred and are used in healing and purification rituals. In Siberian shamanism, drums often have intricate designs and symbols representing the shaman's spiritual journey and connections. These cultural nuances add richness and depth to the practice, showing how diverse yet interconnected shamanic traditions can be.

So, whether you're drumming to the Earth's heartbeat, rattling away stagnant energy, or sending prayers with a feather, remember that these tools are extensions of your intention and spirit. They become powerful allies in your shamanic practice, helping you navigate the spiritual realms with confidence and clarity.

1.6 CREATING A SACRED SPACE: PREPARING FOR SHAMANIC WORK

Imagine trying to meditate in the middle of a noisy café. Sure, the coffee's great, but what about the ambiance? Not so much. This illustrates why creating a sacred space is crucial in shamanic practice. A sacred space is a dedicated area where you can focus, connect with spiritual energies, and perform rituals without distraction. Think of it as your spiritual sanctuary. This place is imbued with your intentions, filled with meaningful objects, and designed to support your shamanic work. The importance of having a dedicated spiritual area cannot be overstated. It allows you to enter a heightened awareness more quickly, providing a safe and sacred environment for your practice.

Creating a sacred space involves several steps. First, choose the correct location. It doesn't have to be a superb room; even a tiny corner of your living room will do. The key is to find a place where you feel comfortable and won't be disturbed. Once you've selected your spot, it's time to cleanse and purify the area. You can smudge with sage, palo santo, or other purifying herbs. You can walk around the space with the smudge stick, allowing the smoke to cleanse the energy. Open windows or doors to let any negative energy escape.

Next, set up an altar with meaningful objects. An altar is the focal point of your sacred space, where you can place items that hold spiritual significance. This could include crystals, feathers, candles, photographs, or anything that resonates with your spiritual practice. Arrange these items in a way that feels harmonious and balanced. The altar becomes a visual and energetic anchor, grounding your intentions and providing a touchstone for your shamanic work.

Symbols and objects play a crucial role in enhancing the sacredness of your space. Crystals, for instance, are not just pretty rocks; they hold specific energies that can amplify your intentions. Feathers symbolize flight and spiritual messages, reminding you of the earthly and divine connection. Other sacred items might include shells, stones, or even a tiny water bowl representing the elements. Each object on your altar should have a purpose and meaning, contributing to the overall energy of the space.

Symbolic representations of the elements can further deepen the sacredness of your space. Incorporate items that represent earth, air, fire, and water to create a balanced and harmonious environment. A small pot of soil or a plant can represent earth, a feather or incense for air, a candle for fire, and a bowl of water for water.

These symbols enhance the energy of your space and serve as reminders of the natural world's interconnectedness and balance.

Maintaining your sacred space is as important as creating it. Regular cleansing rituals help keep the energy clear and vibrant. Smudge the area periodically, and take the time to re-arrange and refresh your altar. Treat this space with respect, as it reflects your spiritual practice. Think of it as a living entity that requires care and attention. Regular maintenance ensures that your sacred space remains a powerful and supportive environment for your shamanic work.

Now, let's add a practical element to this discussion. Consider keeping a journal in your sacred space. This journal can record your experiences, insights, and any messages you receive during your shamanic practices. Writing down your thoughts and reflections can help you track your progress and deepen your understanding of your spiritual journey. It's a simple yet effective way to integrate your experiences and keep your practice grounded.

As you continue to explore the world of shamanism, your sacred space will evolve with you. It will become a sanctuary where you can retreat, connect, and find solace. By dedicating time and effort to create and maintain this space, you honor your spiritual practice and set the stage for profound experiences and insights. So, take a moment, gather your sacred items, and create a space that truly reflects your spirit and intentions. This sacred space will be your sanctuary, place of power, and gateway to the spiritual realms.

CHAPTER 2
PRACTICAL SHAMANIC TECHNIQUES

Not long ago, I sat in my backyard, surrounded by the hum of crickets, the soft glow of lightning bugs, and the cool breeze. I decided it was the perfect moment to take a shamanic journey. I explored the spiritual realms with nothing but my sweat lodge drum and a clear intention. The experience was so profound that I knew I had to share it with you. Welcome to Chapter 2, where we'll dive into practical shamanic techniques, starting with the basic journey.

2.1 HOW TO PERFORM A BASIC SHAMANIC JOURNEY

My teacher, Juan Osco, would say the purpose of a shamanic journey is multifaceted. At its core, it serves as a bridge to the spiritual realms, where you can seek healing, guidance, and insight. Imagine it as a cosmic road trip where you visit places offering profound wisdom and transformative experiences. Journeying allows you to connect with spiritual allies, uncover hidden truths, and bring back valuable insights to enrich your life.

Preparation is key to a successful shamanic journey. Begin by setting a clear intention. What do you hope to achieve? Whether healing an old wound, seeking guidance on a dilemma, or simply exploring the spiritual realms, clarity of purpose will guide your journey. Create a quiet, undisturbed environment. Find a comfortable spot where you won't be interrupted. This might be a cozy corner of your home or a secluded outdoor space. You can enhance the ambiance with sacred sage or incense if you like. These scents can help set the mood and elevate your spiritual experience.

Once your space is ready, focus on relaxation techniques and breathwork. Sit or lie comfortably, close your eyes, and take several deep breaths. Inhale slowly through your nose, letting your belly rise, then exhale through your mouth, releasing any tension. This calms your mind and prepares you for the journey ahead. You might also try progressive muscle relaxation, tensing and relaxing each muscle group, starting from your toes and working your way up to your head.

Now, let's get to the heart of the matter—journeying. Begin by using rhythmic drumming or rattling. The steady beat of a drum or the rhythmic shake of a rattle can help you enter an altered state of consciousness. Imagine the drumbeat as a vehicle transporting you to the spiritual realms. Close your eyes and let the rhythm guide you. Visualization techniques are also essential. Picture yourself at the entrance of a tunnel, a cave, or a staircase leading down into the Lower World or up into the Upper World. The choice of direction depends on your intention. The Lower World is often associated with healing and wisdom, while the Upper World is linked to higher spiritual insights.

As you descend or ascend, engage all your senses. Feel the texture of the ground beneath your feet, hear the sounds of the environment, smell the air, and see the landscape unfold around you. This sensory immersion helps make the journey more vivid and real. Soon, you'll encounter spirit guides or power animals. These benevolent beings offer guidance and support. Approach them with respect and curiosity, asking for their insights and assistance. Trust what you experience, even if your imagination is taking the lead.

Returning from the journey is just as important as the journey itself. Use grounding techniques to ensure a safe return. Visualize roots extending from your body into the Earth, anchoring you firmly. Retrace your steps, returning through the tunnel or staircase you used to enter the spiritual realm. Slowly open your eyes and take a moment to reorient yourself.

Integration is the final step. Take some time to journal your experience. Write down the insights, messages, and any symbols you encountered. This helps solidify the experience and provides a reference for future journeys. Incorporate the insights into your daily life. If your journey revealed a need for more self-care, make time for it. If it offers a solution to a problem, take practical steps to implement it.

To help you get started on your shamanic journey, I've created a simple checklist:

Shamanic Journey Checklist

- Set a clear intention for your journey.
- Create a quiet, undisturbed space.
- Use sacred aromatics to enhance the ambiance (optional).
- Practice relaxation techniques and breathwork.
- Use rhythmic drumming or rattling to enter a trance state.
- Visualize your journey to the Lower or Upper World.
- Engage all your senses during the journey.

- Encounter and interact with spirit guides or power animals.
- You can use grounding techniques to return safely.
- Journal your experience and integrate the insights into daily life.

Ready to start your journey? Find a quiet spot, grab your drum or rattle, and set a clear intention. Remember, the spiritual realms are waiting to offer their wisdom and guidance. Happy journeying!

2.2 CONNECTING WITH YOUR SPIRIT GUIDES

Spirit Guides are like the wise friends and family you didn't know you had, always ready to offer advice and support. In shamanic practice, they play the role of spiritual allies and mentors. These guides can take various forms, from ancestors who have passed on to nature spirits, deities, and even elements of the natural world. Imagine having a team of invisible mentors, each with unique wisdom and abilities, always ready to assist you on your spiritual path. They help navigate life's complexities, offering insights and guidance that can lead to profound personal growth.

Connecting with these spiritual allies involves several techniques. One effective method is meditation. Find a quiet space, sit comfortably, and close your eyes. Focus on your breath, allowing your mind to become peaceful and receptive. Visualize a serene place, such as a forest or a meadow. Invite your spirit guide to join you in this space. Trust the images and sensations that come to you, even if they seem like figments of your imagination. Another technique is invoking spirit guides through rituals. You can light a candle, burn some incense, and speak aloud your intention to connect with your guide if you like. You can also use Dreamwork as a gateway. Before sleep, intend to meet your spirit guide in your dreams. Keep a journal by your bedside to record any messages or symbols you receive upon waking.

Once you've made initial contact, it's very important to strengthen the relationship. Regular communication is key. Treat your spirit guides as you would any valued relationship. Speak to them often through meditation, prayer, or simply talking to them during your daily activities. Offerings can also help solidify this bond. These don't have to be elaborate; simple gestures like lighting a candle, placing fresh flowers, or offering food can show your respect and gratitude. Consider creating a spirit guide altar. This can be a small, dedicated space where you place items representing your guides. It serves as a focal point for your interactions, making it easier to connect with them regularly.

Interpreting messages from spirit guides can sometimes feel like decoding a secret language. They often communicate through symbols and signs that appear in your daily life. Pay attention to recurring patterns, unusual occurrences, or even snippets of conversation that catch your ear. These are often subtle nudges from your guides. Keeping a spirit guide journal can be immensely helpful. Please record your interactions, dreams, and any signs you notice. Over time, you'll start to see patterns and gain a deeper understanding of how your guides communicate. This journal becomes a valuable resource, helping you track your spiritual progress and the guidance you receive.

Understanding the role of spirit guides in your life can lead to profound transformation. They are more than just invisible friends; they are mentors who guide you through life's challenges and help you uncover your true potential. You can cultivate a rich, supportive relationship with these spiritual allies by establishing a solid connection, regularly communicating, and paying attention to their messages. This connection can offer you wisdom, protection, and guidance, enriching your life in ways you might never have imagined.

So, take a moment to sit quietly, close your eyes, and invite your spirit guides into your life. Whether through meditation, rituals, or dream work, these spiritual allies are always ready to support you. With regular practice and an open heart, you can build a strong, lasting relationship with your spirit guides, gaining insights and guidance that can transform your life.

2.3 DISCOVERING YOUR POWER ANIMAL

Power animals are like spiritual sidekicks, always ready to lend a paw, claw, wing, or fin when needed. In shamanic practice, these animals serve as sources of strength and wisdom. They embody qualities that you can draw upon in your daily life, offering guidance and protection. Each power animal has unique attributes that can help you navigate challenges and enhance personal growth. They are symbolic and believed to be real spiritual entities that connect with you deeply.

The cultural significance of power animals varies across different shamanic traditions. In Native American cultures, for example, animals like the eagle and the bear hold significant symbolic meaning and are often seen as messengers from the spirit world. In Siberian shamanism, the reindeer is a revered power animal believed to guide shamans through the harsh tundra. These animals are more than just totems; they are integral to these cultures' spiritual practices and beliefs.

Discovering your power animal involves a spiritual treasure hunt. One effective method is guided visualization. Find a quiet, comfortable place where you won't be disturbed. Close your eyes and take several deep breaths to center yourself. Imagine yourself in a serene, natural environment, perhaps a lush forest or a tranquil meadow. As you walk through this landscape, invite your power animal to reveal itself. Trust what you see, even if it seems like a figment of your imagination. Another method is journeying to the Lower World, a spiritual realm often associated with healing and wisdom. Using rhythmic drumming or rattling, enter a trance state and visualize yourself descending into this realm. As you explore, you may encounter your power animal. Approach it with respect and curiosity, asking for its guidance and support.

Once you've identified your power animal, it's time to build a relationship with it. This isn't a one-time introduction but an ongoing friendship. Daily rituals and meditations can strengthen this bond. Spend a few minutes connecting with your power animal through visualization or talking to it daily. Creating art or symbols representing your power animal can also deepen your connection. Draw pictures, make sculptures, or even write stories featuring your animal. These creative expressions serve as reminders of the qualities your power animal embodies. Regularly seeking guidance from your power animal is another way to maintain this relationship. Call upon your power animal for support and wisdom when faced with challenges or decisions.

Utilizing the wisdom and strength of your power animal can profoundly impact your daily life. You can call upon your power animal for courage and guidance in difficult situations. For instance, if your power animal is a lion, you might draw upon its strength and bravery when facing a daunting task. If your power animal is an owl, seek its wisdom and clarity when making a tough decision. Incorporating your power animal's teachings into your personal growth can also be transformative. I'd like you to reflect on the qualities your power animal represents and how they can enhance your life. If your power animal is a turtle, its slow and steady nature might teach you the value of patience and perseverance. If it's a butterfly, its metamorphosis might inspire you to embrace change and transformation.

To help you get started, here's a simple exercise:

Power Animal Connection Exercise

1. Find a quiet, comfortable place where you won't be disturbed.
2. Close your eyes and take several deep breaths to center yourself.
3. Visualize yourself in a forest, meadow, or beach.
4. As you walk through this landscape, invite your power animal to reveal itself.
5. Pay attention to any animals that appear, even if they seem like figments of your imagination.
6. Approach the animal with respect and curiosity, asking for guidance and support.
7. Spend a few minutes connecting with your power animal, then slowly return to your surroundings.

By incorporating the wisdom and strength of your power animal into your daily life, you can navigate challenges with greater ease and confidence. This spiritual ally offers you a unique perspective and a source of support, enriching your shamanic practice and personal growth. So, please take a moment to connect with your power animal and let its wisdom guide you on your path.

2.4 SHAMANIC DRUMMING TECHNIQUES FOR BEGINNERS

Drumming holds a special place in shamanic practice, akin to the heartbeat of the Earth. It's more than just a rhythmic activity; it's a powerful tool for entering trance states. When you drum, you make noise and create a rhythmic bridge to the spiritual realms. The repetitive beat helps quiet the mind, allowing you to slip into an altered state of consciousness where profound insights and healing can occur. Think of it as tuning into the Earth's natural frequency, aligning yourself with its rhythms and vibrations.

Now, let's talk technique. Holding the drum correctly is the first step. If using a frame drum, rest it on your non-dominant hand, letting it balance comfortably. Use your dominant hand to strike the drum head. How you hold the drum can affect the sound and your comfort during extended drumming sessions. Aim for the center to produce a deep, resonant sound when striking the drum. If you're using a drumstick, hold it loosely to allow for a natural bounce. Basic rhythms for journeying are usually simple and repetitive. A steady, monotonous beat is most effective for entering trance states. Start with a slow, consistent rhythm, gradually increasing the speed if it feels right. Consistency is vital, so please practice maintaining the same beat for several minutes.

Creating a regular drumming practice can be incredibly rewarding. You can start by setting up a dedicated drumming space. This could be a corner of your room or a spot in your garden—anywhere you feel comfortable and won't be disturbed. Decorate this space with items that inspire you, such as candles, crystals, or meaningful symbols. Developing a daily drumming routine can deepen your connection to the practice. Aim for at least 10–15 minutes of drumming each day. Over time, you'll find it easier to enter trance states and receive the benefits of shamanic drumming. Consistency is your friend here; the more you practice, the more intuitive it will become.

Drumming with intention is another crucial aspect of the practice. Before you start, set a clear intention for your session. Are you drumming for healing, seeking guidance, or exploring the spiritual realms? Having a focused intention can enhance the effectiveness of your drumming. As you drum, keep this intention in mind. Let the rhythm guide you, but please keep in mind your purpose. This focused approach can make your sessions more meaningful and impactful.

Shamanic drumming isn't just about making noise; it's a sacred practice that connects you to deeper spiritual realms. By holding the drum correctly, maintaining basic rhythms, and setting clear intentions, you can transform your drumming sessions into powerful spiritual experiences. Your dedicated drumming space becomes a sanctuary where you can explore these realms, gaining insights and healing. So grab your drum, find your rhythm, and let the journey begin.

2.5 GUIDED MEDITATION FOR SHAMANIC PRACTICE

Meditation in shamanism is like the Swiss Army knife of spiritual tools. It's incredibly versatile, offering everything from inner stillness to profound clarity. Consider meditation as the mental warm-up before diving into more intensive shamanic practices. It prepares your mind, making it a fertile ground for spiritual work. When your mind is calm and focused, you're better equipped to navigate the spiritual realms, whether you're seeking healing, guidance, or insight. Meditation helps you center yourself, creating a state of inner stillness where the chatter of daily life fades away, leaving space for more profound spiritual experiences.

Let's talk about some guided meditation techniques tailored for shamanic purposes. One fundamental practice is grounding meditation. Imagine roots growing from your feet, burrowing deep into the Earth. This visualization helps you connect with the Earth's energy, providing a stable foundation for your spiritual work. Feel the Earth's nurturing energy rise through these roots, filling you with balance and stability. Grounding is beneficial when you feel scattered or overwhelmed, anchoring you back to the present moment.

Visualization meditation is another powerful technique. Picture yourself in a serene natural setting—a forest, a beach, or a mountain. Invite your spirit guide to join you in this tranquil place. Visualize the guide approaching you, offering wisdom and support. This practice helps you establish and deepen your connection with your spiritual allies. The key is to engage all your senses. Hear the rustling leaves, feel the breeze on your skin, and see the vivid colors of your surroundings. This sensory immersion makes the experience more real and impactful.

Healing meditation focuses on balancing your energy. Close your eyes and take deep breaths. Visualize a warm, golden light enveloping your body. This light represents healing energy, cleansing, and balancing your chakras. As you breathe in, imagine this light filling you with positive energy. As you exhale, release any negativity or tension. This practice can be particularly effective when feeling out of sorts or emotionally drained. It's like giving your energy field a spa day, leaving you refreshed and rejuvenated.

Creating a meditation space is crucial for effective practice. You can choose a quiet, comfortable location where you won't be disturbed. This could be a dedicated room, a corner of your bedroom, or even a spot in your garden. The key is to make it a place where you feel at ease. Enhance the ambiance with candles, incense, or sacred objects. These elements can help you set the mood and elevate your meditation practice. Think of this space as your sanctuary, where you can retreat from the hustle and bustle of daily life and focus on your spiritual growth.

Incorporating meditation into your daily life doesn't have to be a chore. Short daily practices can be incredibly effective. Even five to ten minutes of meditation daily can make a significant difference. Start your day with a quick grounding meditation, or end it with a visualization practice to connect with your spirit guides. Combining meditation with other shamanic practices can also enhance your overall experience. For instance, you might meditate before a shamanic journey or after a drumming session. The goal is to make meditation a regular part of your routine, seamlessly integrating it into your daily life.

To help you get started, here's a simple meditation script:

Close your eyes and take a deep breath. Imagine yourself in a peaceful forest. The air is fresh, and the sounds of nature surround you. Feel the ground beneath your feet, solid and reassuring. Now, visualize roots growing from your feet, reaching deep into the Earth. With each breath, feel the Earth's energy rising through these roots, filling you with stability and balance. As you exhale, release any tension or negative energy. Continue this breathing pattern for a few minutes, allowing yourself to become fully grounded and centered. When you're ready, slowly open your eyes, bringing this sense of calm and balance into your day.

Meditation is a cornerstone of shamanic practice, offering a way to prepare your mind, connect with spiritual allies, and balance your energy. Creating a conducive environment and incorporating short daily practices make meditation integral to your spiritual journey. So, find a quiet spot, light a candle, and let the meditation begin.

2.6 SETTING UP AND USING AN ALTAR

The significance of having an altar, mesa, or bundle in shamanic practice cannot be overstated. An altar is the focal point for your spiritual work, anchoring your intentions and creating a sacred space for rituals and offerings. Think of it as your spiritual workstation. This is where the magic happens, where you connect with the divine and align yourself with the universe's energies. An altar lets you focus your spiritual activities, making slipping into a meditative or trance state easier. It's a place to lay out your tools, symbols, and offerings, creating a tangible representation of your spiritual practice.

Setting up an altar is a deeply personal process that allows you to express your spirituality in a physical form. First, you can select a location that feels right. If you prefer to connect directly with nature, this could be a quiet corner of your room, a dedicated table, or even a spot outdoors. The key is to find a place where you feel comfortable and won't be disturbed during your rituals. Once you've chosen your spot, start gathering meaningful objects and symbols. These could include crystals, feathers, candles, photographs, or any items that hold spiritual significance for you. Arrange these items with intention and purpose. For example, you might place a crystal in the center to represent balance or a feather to signify communication with the spirit world. The arrangement should feel harmonious and resonate with you on a deep level.

Using the altar for rituals and offerings is where the practice becomes interactive. Making offerings to your spirit guides and power animals can be as simple or elaborate as you like. You might light a candle, place fresh flowers, or offer a small amount of food. The key is to do so with intention and respect. Regular offerings show gratitude and help maintain a strong connection with your spiritual allies. Performing rituals and ceremonies at the altar can also enhance your practice. Whether you're conducting an entire moon ceremony, a healing ritual, or simply meditating, the altar serves as a powerful focal point. It's a place to channel your energy and intentions, making your rituals more effective and meaningful.

Maintaining and evolving your altar is an ongoing process. It requires regular upkeep to keep it energetically clear and vibrant, like any space. Make it a habit to clean your altar regularly, dust off items, and refresh offerings. This keeps the space physically clean and maintains its energetic integrity. Changing items on your altar seasonally or as guided by intuition can also keep the energy fresh. For instance, add flowers in the spring, leaves in the fall, or crystals that resonate with the current season. Your altar is a living entity, evolving with your spiritual practice. I want to point out that regularly updating it makes sure it stays aligned with your current intentions and needs.

So, whether you're a seasoned practitioner or new to shamanism, setting up an altar can significantly enhance your practice. It's a sacred space where you can ground your intentions, connect with spiritual allies, and perform rituals that bring about profound transformation. By keeping it clean, updating it regularly, and using it with intention, you create a powerful tool for your spiritual journey. An altar is more than just a collection of objects; it's a gateway to the divine, where the physical and spiritual worlds intersect.

In this chapter, we've explored various practical techniques to deepen your shamanic practice, from journeying and connecting with spirit guides to discovering power animals and using drumming. These methods offer a solid foundation for any beginner, helping you navigate the complexities of shamanic work. Next, we'll dive into the healing aspects of shamanism, exploring how these ancient practices can bring about profound physical, emotional, and spiritual healing. Get ready to unlock the transformative power of shamanic healing techniques in the coming chapters.

CHAPTER 3

HEALING PRACTICES IN SHAMANISM

3.1 THE ART OF SOUL RETRIEVAL

Picture this: you're going about your day, feeling a bit off, like you've left your keys somewhere but need help remembering where. What if I told you that this feeling might not be about your keys but pieces of your soul that have gone missing? This brings us to shamanism's intriguing concept of soul loss and retrieval. Soul loss occurs when parts of your soul fragment and leave due to trauma or intense emotional experiences. Imagine pieces of yourself wandering off to avoid the pain, leaving you feeling incomplete or disconnected. This isn't just poetic language; it's a core belief in shamanism.

Soul retrieval is a crucial shamanic healing practice to reclaim these lost soul fragments. Think of it as a spiritual scavenger hunt, where the goal is to gather all the missing pieces and make you whole again. This practice is essential for holistic healing, addressing not just physical and emotional wounds but also the spiritual gaps that can linger long after the initial trauma. You can restore your sense of wholeness, balance, and vitality by retrieving these lost parts. It's like finally finding all the missing pieces of a puzzle, allowing you to see the complete picture of yourself.

The process of soul retrieval is both fascinating and methodical. It begins with preparation. As a shamanic practitioner, you must enter an altered state of consciousness, often achieved through drumming, rattling, or deep meditation. This state allows you to navigate the spiritual realms where the soul fragments reside. Before you begin this journey, setting a clear intention and calling upon your spirit guides for help is crucial. These guides act as your spiritual GPS, helping you locate the lost soul parts. They offer protection and guidance, ensuring you navigate the spiritual realms safely and effectively.

Once in the spiritual realm, the task is to locate and retrieve the lost soul parts. This isn't as simple as shouting, "Marco!" and waiting for a "Polo!" in response. It involves deep intuition and spiritual navigation. You might visualize these soul parts as luminous orbs or even as younger versions of yourself. When you find a fragment, invite it to return with you, reassuring it that it's safe and welcome. This invitation is crucial; the soul part needs to feel secure enough to reintegrate. Once you've gathered all the fragments, you return to the physical realm and perform a ritual to reintegrate these parts into your being. This ritual could involve visualization, breath work, or even a symbolic act like lighting a candle.

Identifying signs of soul loss can help determine if you or someone you know might benefit from soul retrieval. Common symptoms include feeling incomplete, chronic fatigue, depression, or a sense of disconnection from life. You might also experience unexplained bouts of sadness or anger or feel like you're just going through the motions without truly living. These symptoms are indicators that parts of your soul might be missing, stuck in the past, or unable to move forward.

The benefits of soul retrieval are profound. Emotionally, it can lead to a sense of completeness and peace with oneself and one's past. Spiritually, it enhances your connection to yourself and the world, making you feel more grounded and present. Physically, you might notice increased energy and vitality. It's like upgrading your operating system, making everything run smoother and more efficiently.

I'd like to share some real-life examples to show the transformative power of soul retrieval. One of my clients, Sarah, came to me feeling perpetually exhausted and disconnected. She had experienced a series of traumatic events that left her feeling fragmented. During a soul retrieval session, we located several lost soul parts, each associated with a specific trauma. After reintegrating these parts, Sarah reported feeling renewed energy and wholeness. She described it as if she had finally come home to herself. Another client, John, had struggled with chronic sadness and a feeling of emptiness. Through soul retrieval, we discovered that parts of his soul had fragmented during a difficult childhood. Reclaiming these parts brought about a profound emotional healing, allowing John to move forward with a newfound sense of peace and joy.

Case Study: Sarah's Transformation

Sarah's journey began with a sense of perpetual exhaustion and disconnection. She felt like she was sleepwalking through life, unable to engage or find joyfully. After a series of traumatic events, she sought help through shamanic soul retrieval. During the sessions, we identified and retrieved several lost soul parts, each linked to a specific trauma. The reintegration process was transformative. Sarah described feeling a surge of energy and a deep sense of wholeness. She said it was like pieces of her that had been missing for years finally came home. This newfound vitality allowed her to pursue her passions and fully engage with life.

Soul retrieval is a powerful tool for healing and personal transformation. By addressing the spiritual aspects of trauma, it offers a holistic approach to healing that encompasses the physical, emotional, and spiritual dimensions of well-being. So, if you've ever felt something essential is missing from your life, it might be worth exploring the art of soul retrieval. It's a journey back to wholeness, guided by ancient wisdom and the compassionate support of spirit guides.

3.2 ENERGY WORK: BALANCING AND HEALING YOUR ENERGY FIELD

Imagine your energy field as a finely tuned orchestra. When every instrument plays in harmony, the result is a beautiful symphony. But if even one instrument is off-key, the entire performance suffers. This analogy explains why maintaining a balanced energy field is crucial for well-being. Energy work in shamanism focuses on keeping this symphony in tune. It addresses the flow and balance of energy within and around you, ensuring that you function at your highest potential. Energy balance is vital because it impacts physical health, emotional stability, and spiritual clarity.

Smudging with sage or other sacred herbs is one effective technique for cleansing and balancing your energy. Picture this: you're standing in your living room, feeling sluggish and out of sorts. You light a bundle of sage and let the smoke move around you, visualizing it sweeping away any negative or stagnant energy. Sage's scent is calming and invigorating, making it easier to enter a relaxed state. This simple act can refresh and revitalize you, like opening a window to let in the fresh air.

Visualization techniques also play a significant role in energy cleansing. Imagine a golden light surrounding your body, enveloping you in warmth and positivity. As you breathe in, visualize this light filling your entire being, pushing out any darkness or negativity. Exhale and see the dark energy dissipate into the ether. Repeat this process several times until you feel lighter and more balanced. Visualization is powerful because it engages your mind and spirit, making the cleansing process more effective.

Crystals are another valuable aid in energy work. Different crystals have unique properties that can help balance your energy field. For example, amethyst is known for its calming and protective qualities, while rose quartz promotes love and emotional healing. To use crystals, hold one in your hand during meditation or place it on different parts of your body that need healing. You can also create a crystal grid around your space, enhancing the overall energy of the environment.

In shamanic healing, chakras are crucial energy centers within the body. Think of them as spinning wheels of energy, each corresponding to your physical, emotional, and spiritual well-being. There are seven main chakras, from the spine's base to the head's crown. Each chakra has its unique color and function. For instance, the root chakra, located at the base of the spine, is associated with grounding and security, while the heart chakra, in the center of the chest, deals with love and compassion.

Balancing these chakras can lead to profound healing. One effective technique is chakra meditation. Sit comfortably and close your eyes. Focus on each chakra, starting from the root and moving up to the crown. Visualize each chakra as a spinning wheel of light, its color glowing brightly. If a chakra feels blocked or dim, imagine it being cleansed and revitalized by a stream of pure energy. This process can help restore balance and harmony to your entire energy system.

Daily energy cleansing rituals can be simple yet effective. Start your day by taking a few moments to ground yourself. Stand firmly planted on the ground, close your eyes, and take deep breaths. Visualize roots extending from your feet into the Earth, anchoring you firmly. This grounding exercise helps you start the day with stability and balance. In the evening, cleanse your energy by visualizing a shower of golden light washing over you, removing any stress or negativity accumulated throughout the day.

Guided meditations for energy alignment can also be incredibly beneficial. Find a quiet space where you won't be disturbed. Close your eyes and take several deep breaths. Visualize a column of light extending from the top of your head to the base of your spine. Imagine this light aligning all your chakras, bringing them into perfect harmony. Please spend a few minutes focusing on each chakra, visualizing it spinning brightly and freely. This meditation can leave you feeling balanced, centered, and ready to face whatever comes your way. Energy work is a versatile and powerful tool in shamanic healing. You can maintain a harmonious energy field by incorporating techniques like smudging, visualization, and chakra balancing into your daily routine. This balance is essential for physical health, emotional stability, and spiritual clarity. So, take a moment to tune your energy orchestra and enjoy the beautiful symphony of a balanced life.

3.3 SHAMANIC HEALING WITH NATURE'S ELEMENTS

Imagine standing barefoot on the earth, feeling the cool ground beneath your feet, the wind rustling through the trees, the warmth of the sun on your skin, and the sound of a flowing river nearby. These elements – earth, air, fire, and water – are not just the building blocks of nature but also powerful tools in shamanic healing practices. Each element carries unique healing properties and plays a specific role in shamanic rituals.

Earth Mother is the great stabilizer. It grounds us, providing a sense of security and stability. In shamanic practices, working with the earth involves grounding techniques and using stones for healing. Picture yourself holding a smooth stone while sitting on the ground. Close your eyes and imagine roots extending from your body into the earth, anchoring you firmly. This simple act can help you feel more centered and balanced. Stones and crystals, with their unique energies, are also used in healing rituals. Place a grounding stone-like hematite on your root chakra to stabilize your energy and foster a sense of safety.

Air is the breath of life, symbolizing intellect and communication. In shamanic practices, breathwork and using feathers for cleansing are common. Imagine taking deep, deliberate breaths, filling your lungs with fresh air, and then exhaling slowly, releasing tension or negativity. This breath work can help clear your mind and energize your body. Feathers are also used to cleanse the energy field. Picture yourself gently waving a feather around your body, visualizing it sweeping away any stagnant energy and leaving you feeling refreshed and invigorated.

Fire is the element of transformation, representing passion and creative action. In shamanic rituals, fire ceremonies and candle rituals harness this transformative power. Imagine lighting a candle with a specific intention, such as releasing old patterns or igniting new beginnings. As the flame flickers, visualize it burning away what no longer serves you and illuminating your path forward. Fire ceremonies, where participants gather around a bonfire, offer a communal way to release the old and welcome the new. Write down what you wish to release on paper and throw it into the fire, watching it turn ash and feel the liberation it brings.

Water, the element of emotions and intuition, is soothing and purifying. Healing baths and rituals by natural water sources harness the power of water. Imagine soaking in a warm bath infused with healing herbs or essential oils, feeling the water wash away stress and negative energy. Visualize the water absorbing your worries, leaving you feeling calm and rejuvenated. Rituals by rivers, lakes, or the ocean also offer profound healing. Picture yourself standing by a flowing river, tossing a stone into the water as a symbol of releasing negativity and watching it carried away by the current.

Seasonal and environmental awareness plays a significant role in shamanic healing practices. The changing seasons and local environment influence the energies we work with. Aligning your practices with seasonal cycles can enhance their effectiveness. In spring, focus on renewal and growth, planting seeds in a ritual to symbolize new beginnings. With its vibrant energy, summer is perfect for celebrating life and abundance. Fall encourages introspection and letting go, while winter is a time for rest and reflection. Using local natural resources, like herbs and stones from your surroundings, can also deepen your connection to the land and enhance your healing practices.

Let me share a few personal stories to illustrate the power of healing with nature's elements. A client of mine, struggling with anxiety, found solace in a simple grounding ritual. She would sit on the earth, holding a grounding stone, and imagine roots extending from her body into the ground. This practice helped her feel more stable and secure, reducing her anxiety significantly. A student of mine, dealing with emotional turmoil, found great relief in water rituals. She would visit a local river and commune with a great blue heron, release her worries into the water, and feel the current carry them away. Letting go brought her a sense of peace and emotional clarity.

Working with nature's elements in shamanic healing practices offers a deeply holistic approach to well-being. By connecting with the earth, air, fire, and water, you can harness their unique properties to heal and transform. Whether grounding yourself with the earth, cleansing with air, transforming with fire, or purifying with water, these elements enhance your spiritual practice and overall well-being. So, take a moment to connect with the natural world around you and explore the healing power of nature's elements.

3.4 PLANT MEDICINE: AN INTRODUCTION TO SACRED PLANTS

Imagine sipping a brew that opens the door to another dimension, where the universe whispers its secrets, and you find yourself face-to-face with ancient wisdom. Welcome to the world of plant medicine in shamanism. Sacred plants have played a pivotal role in shamanic healing, bridging the physical and spiritual realms. These plants are not just flora but revered allies in the shamanic practice, carrying centuries of cultural significance and spiritual power. The history of plant medicine in shamanism dates back to ancient civilizations where shamans and healers used these plants to induce visions, heal ailments, and connect with the divine. These plants are considered sacred because of their ability to alter consciousness and facilitate profound healing and spiritual experiences.

Different cultures have unique sacred plants, each with specific uses and significance. Ayahuasca, often called the "vine of the soul," is a potent brew that the Amazonian tribes used for spiritual healing and visionary experiences. This plant medicine is known for its ability to provide deep insights, emotional healing, and a sense of connection to the cosmos. Peyote, a small cactus native to the southwestern United States and Mexico, has been used for centuries by Native American tribes in ceremonial contexts. It induces altered states of consciousness, allowing participants to connect with spiritual realms, gain insights, and heal emotional wounds. These plants are not just tools but are seen as teachers, guiding users through transformative experiences.

The benefits and healing properties of these sacred plants are profound. Ayahuasca, for instance, is known for its ability to purge negative energies and emotions, leading to emotional and spiritual healing. Many users report a sense of clarity and purpose after an ayahuasca ceremony, as well as relief from conditions like depression and anxiety. Conversely, Peyote is revered for its ability to provide spiritual insights and emotional healing. Participants in peyote ceremonies often describe experiencing a deep sense of peace, connection, and understanding. However, the use of these plants comes with ethical considerations. It's crucial to approach them with respect and cultural sensitivity. Many indigenous communities have strict protocols for using these plants, and it's essential to honor these traditions to avoid cultural appropriation and exploitation.

Preparing and using plant medicine responsibly requires a respectful and mindful approach. Rituals for preparing plant medicine are integral to the process. For instance, the preparation of ayahuasca involves a meticulous process of combining specific plants and boiling them for hours, often accompanied by prayers and intentions. This preparation is done in a sacred space, acknowledging the spirit of the plant and setting the stage for the healing experience. When using these plants, doing so safely and respectfully is crucial. Please make sure you are in a supportive environment, preferably under the guidance of an experienced shaman or facilitator. Respect plant medicine as a sacred ally, not as a recreational substance. You can set clear intentions for your experience and approach it with an open heart and mind.

To give you a deeper understanding, let's look at some stories and insights from practitioners who have used plant medicine for healing. One practitioner, Dawn of The New Era, a shamanic energy healer, describes her experiences with ayahuasca as life-changing. She shares how the plant medicine opened her heart and helped her confront past traumas, leading to a sense of freedom and peace with herself and a part of her past. Another participant in a peyote ceremony described the experience as a profound spiritual journey that provided clarity and guidance for his life's path; he spoke of feeling deeply connected to his ancestors and gaining insights that helped him navigate personal challenges.

Case Study: Kate's Experience

Kate, a shamanic student, recounts her transformative experiences with ayahuasca. She describes how the plant medicine helped her confront and heal deep-seated emotional PTSD. The ceremonies, conducted in a sacred space with experienced shamans, gave her a sense of security and peace with herself and her past. Kate emphasizes the importance of ceremonies that help you prepare before approaching plant medicine with respect and cultural sensitivity, honoring the traditions of the indigenous communities who have used these plants for centuries.

These testimonials highlight the transformative power of plant medicine when used responsibly and respectfully. They offer a glimpse into the profound healing and spiritual insights that these sacred plants can provide. Whether through ayahuasca, peyote, or other sacred plants, the journey with plant medicine can be a transformative experience, offering deep healing and spiritual growth.

3.5 HEALING THROUGH SOUND: USING DRUMS AND RATTLES

Imagine sitting in a circle, the rhythmic beat of drums reverberating through your body. The vibrations penetrate your soul, creating a sense of unity and healing. In shamanic practice, sound is not just an auditory experience; it's a powerful tool for healing and transformation. Sound vibrations can influence your energy field, breaking stagnant energy and facilitating emotional release. The importance of sound in healing lies in its ability to affect every cell in your body, creating a harmonious environment for healing to occur. Drums and rattles are central to this practice, each offering unique benefits.

Drums often induce trance states and facilitate healing with deep, resonant tones. The repetitive beat of the drum can help you enter a meditative state, where healing can take place on a profound level. Conversely, rattles produce a sharp, percussive sound that can break up stagnant energy and clear your energy field. Imagine using a rattle to sweep away negative energy, much like a broom to clean a dusty floor. The sound of the rattle disrupts the stagnant energy, allowing fresh, positive energy to flow in.

Using drums and rattles for healing involves specific techniques tailored to different needs. For instance, if you're seeking emotional release, you might use a slow, steady drumbeat to help you enter a deep meditative state. Picture yourself sitting comfortably, eyes closed, as you strike the drum with a rhythmic, deliberate beat. Allow the sound to wash over you, focusing on the areas where you feel emotional tension. The vibrations help to loosen and release these emotions, facilitating healing. A rattle can be incredibly effective in clearing your energy field. Stand in a relaxed position, holding the rattle in one hand. Shake it around your body, focusing on heavy or blocked areas. Visualize the sound, breaking up the stagnant energy and replacing it with light and vitality.

Creating a sound healing practice involves more than picking up a drum or rattle. It's about setting up a sacred space to focus on your healing work. Choose a quiet, comfortable area where you won't be disturbed. Decorate this space with items that inspire you, such as candles, crystals, or meaningful symbols. This sacred space becomes a sanctuary for your sound healing practice, enhancing its effectiveness. Combining sound healing with other shamanic practices can also amplify its benefits. For instance, you might begin with a grounding meditation and a drumming session to deepen your relaxation. Incorporating breathwork or visualization techniques can further enhance the healing experience.

Real-life stories highlight the transformative power of sound healing. Take, for example, a client named Kelly, who struggled with stress and anxiety. She began incorporating drumming into her daily routine, spending just 15 minutes each morning in her sacred space. The rhythmic beat of the drum helped her enter a meditative state, releasing her stress and calming her mind. Over time, Kelly noticed a significant reduction in her anxiety levels and an overall sense of well-being. Another client, Tony, used rattling to clear his energy field after a particularly challenging period. He found that the sharp, percussive sound of the rattle helped him release negative energy and regain a sense of peace. Tony described the experience as a "spiritual reboot," leaving him feeling clear and more focused.

Case Study: Kelly's Transformation

Kelly, a high-stressed energy worker, found peace in sound healing. She incorporated drumming into her daily routine, dedicating 15 minutes each morning to this practice. In her sacred space, surrounded by plants, candles, crystals, and singing bowls, Kelly would lose herself in the rhythmic beat of the drum. This simple act helped her enter a meditative state, releasing her stress and calming her mind. Over time, Kelly's stress levels decreased significantly, and she experienced an overall sense of well-being. Her story is a testament to the transformative power of sound healing in shamanic practice.

Sound healing through drums and rattles offers a profound way to balance your energy and facilitate healing. By incorporating these practices into your routine, you can experience the transformative power of sound, enhancing your physical, emotional, and spiritual well-being. So, find your rhythm, create your sacred space, and let the healing vibrations of sound guide you to a state of harmony and balance.

3.6 THE ROLE OF CEREMONY IN SHAMANIC HEALING

Ceremonies are pivotal in shamanic healing as gateways to the spiritual realm. Imagine them as bridges connecting the physical and spiritual worlds, allowing us to traverse back and forth, gathering wisdom and healing energy. Through ritual and sacred acts, ceremonies create a space where the ordinary meets the extraordinary, offering profound opportunities for transformation. They are not mere performances but deeply intentional practices designed to invoke the presence of spirits, ancestors, and other spiritual allies.

Shamanic ceremonies come in many forms, each serving a unique purpose. Healing ceremonies, for example, are designed to restore balance and harmony within individuals and communities. These ceremonies may involve chanting, drumming, and using sacred tools to invoke healing energies. Seasonal and cyclical rituals, on the other hand, align us with the Earth's natural rhythms. Think of rituals celebrating the solstices or equinoxes, where the community gathers to honor the changing seasons and seek blessings for the months ahead. These ceremonies help us stay connected to the natural cycles and remind us of our place within the larger web of life.

Creating and conducting effective shamanic ceremonies involves several key steps. Preparation is crucial. You can begin by setting a clear intention for the ceremony. What do you hope to achieve? Whether it's healing, guidance, or celebration, a focused intention will guide the entire process. Next, create a sacred atmosphere. Choose a location that feels right, whether outdoors in nature or in a quiet indoor space. Cleanse the area with sage or other purifying herbs to clear any negative energy. Arrange your sacred tools and symbols in a harmonious and meaningful way.

The elements of a successful ceremony include invoking the presence of spirit guides and allies, setting up an altar with meaningful objects, and using sounds, such as drumming or chanting, to enter a meditative state. Involving participants is also essential. Encourage those present to set their intentions and actively engage in the ritual. This could include offering prayers, symbolic gestures, or guided meditations. The group's energy can amplify the ceremony's power, creating a collective field of healing and transformation.

Let's explore some personal stories and cultural insights that highlight the power of ceremony. In many indigenous cultures, ceremonies are deeply woven into the fabric of daily life. For example, the Nemenhah people perform the Winter Dance, a powerful healing and renewal ceremony that involves dancing, fasting, and prayer. This ceremony is a communal act of devotion and sacrifice of dancing, aimed at seeking visions and blessings from the ancestors for the entire community and bountiful spring rains. Another example comes from Peru, where Ayahuasca ceremonies facilitate spiritual healing and visionary experiences and heal past traumas. Participants drink a sacred brew and engage in rituals led by a shaman, who guides them through the journey, helping them navigate the spiritual realms and interpret and integrate their experiences.

One personal story that stands out involves a community healing ceremony I facilitated. A group of individuals, each carrying their burdens and traumas, gathered in a circle, united by a common intention to heal. We started with a cleansing ritual, using sage to purify the space and ourselves. Participants were invited to share their intentions, creating a collective field of vulnerability and openness. As the drumming began, we meditated, calling upon our spirit guides for assistance. The energy in the room was palpable, a mix of anticipation and reverence. By the end of the ceremony, many participants reported feeling a profound sense of release and renewal, as if a heavy weight had been lifted.

Cultural perspectives on ritual and healing vary, but the underlying principles remain consistent: ceremonies are a way to connect with the divine, seek guidance, and facilitate healing. In Tibetan Buddhism, for example, ceremonies often involve intricate rituals and offerings aimed at invoking the presence of deities and receiving their blessings. These rituals are symbolic and believed to create fundamental changes in the spiritual and physical realms. Similarly, in African shamanic traditions, ceremonies often involve drumming, dancing, and using sacred objects to invoke the presence of ancestors and spirits. These rituals are a way to honor the past, seek guidance for the present, and ensure blessings for the future.

The importance of ceremony in shamanic healing cannot be overstated. They provide a structured yet flexible framework for engaging with the spiritual realms, offering profound transformation and healing opportunities. By understanding the different types of ceremonies and learning how to create and conduct them effectively, you can harness their power to enrich your spiritual practice and enhance your overall well-being. Whether you're performing a simple personal ritual or a complex community ceremony, the principles remain the same: intention, preparation, and active participation. So, take a moment to reflect on the role of ceremony in your own life and consider how you might incorporate these powerful practices into your spiritual journey.

Ceremonies offer a structured yet flexible approach to connecting with the spiritual realms and facilitating profound healing and transformation. Whether performing a simple personal ritual or a complex community ceremony, understanding the principles of intention, preparation, and participation can enhance your practice. This chapter has explored various shamanic healing practices, each offering unique insights and techniques for personal and communal healing. In the next chapter, we'll delve into the cultural context and authenticity of shamanic practices, exploring how to honor and respect the rich traditions that form the foundation of shamanism.

CHAPTER 4
CULTURAL CONTEXT AND AUTHENTICITY

Picture this: you're gazing at a prehistoric cave painting at a museum. The figures seem to dance on the walls, depicting rituals and ceremonies from a world long gone. These ancient artworks aren't just doodles from bored cave dwellers; they are among the earliest evidence of shamanic practices. As you'll discover, Shamanism has roots that stretch back to the dawn of human history, evolving uniquely across various cultures.

4.1 THE HISTORY OF SHAMANISM ACROSS CULTURES

Shamanic practices originated in prehistoric times, as evidenced by cave paintings in places like Lascaux, France, and Altamira, Spain. These ancient artworks depict figures engaged in rituals, often adorned with animal skins and masks. These early shamans acted as intermediaries between the physical and spiritual realms, guiding their communities through life's and death's mysteries. In hunter-gatherer societies, shamans played a crucial role. They were the healers, the spiritual leaders, and the keepers of wisdom. Imagine living in a world where every aspect of life is infused with spiritual significance, and the shaman is the one who can navigate these unseen realms.

Shamanism isn't a one-size-fits-all practice; it has been uniquely adapted and interpreted across different cultures. Take Siberia, for example, which is often considered the birthplace of shamanism. Siberian shamans, or "Tungus," are known for their elaborate rituals involving drumming, chanting, and intricate costumes adorned with bells and feathers. These shamans' journey to the spirit world to seek guidance and healing for their community. In Native American cultures, the role of the shaman, or medicine person, is equally vital. Their practices often involve rituals to honor the spirits of nature, such as the Sun Dance or the Vision Quest, where individuals seek personal insights and spiritual guidance. South American shamanic traditions, particularly among Amazonian tribes, involve using plant medicine like Ayahuasca. These practices are deeply rooted in the belief that plants have spirits that can offer profound healing and wisdom.

While shamanic practices vary widely, they share several universal elements. Spirit journeying, for instance, is a common thread. Shamans enter altered states of consciousness to travel to the spirit world through drumming, chanting, or using sacred plants. Healing is another core aspect. Shamans act as healers, connecting to the spiritual realm to diagnose and treat ailments. Rituals, often involving sacred tools like drums, rattles, and feathers, are also a standard feature. However, the specific tools and practices can vary significantly. Siberian shamans might use elaborate costumes and drum rhythms, while Amazonian shamans rely on plant medicines and chanting.

Consider the role of the shaman in ancient Mongolian societies. Mongolian shamans, known as "boo," played a central role in their communities, conducting rituals to communicate with spirits and ancestors. These rituals often involved drumming, singing, and using sacred objects like mirrors and swords. Historical accounts from Africa also provide fascinating insights into shamanic healing ceremonies. In many African cultures, shamans are known as "sangomas" or "ngangas." They use a combination of drumming, dancing, and herbal medicine to heal and guide their communities. One historical account describes a healing ceremony where a sangoma, adorned in vibrant beads and animal skins, danced and chanted to invoke the spirits, ultimately healing a sick child.

Reflection Exercise: Exploring Your Cultural Connection

Take a moment to reflect on the cultural context of shamanism. Consider the following questions:

1. What aspects of shamanic practices resonate most with you?
2. Are there any cultural traditions or practices from your heritage that align with shamanic principles?
3. How can you incorporate these elements into your spiritual practice while honoring their cultural origins?

I'd like you to write down your thoughts in a journal. This exercise can help you deepen your understanding and connection to the rich tapestry of shamanic traditions across cultures.

In its many forms, Shamanism offers a fascinating glimpse into the spiritual practices that have shaped human history. By understanding its origins and cultural variations, you can appreciate the depth and diversity of this ancient tradition. Whether you're drawn to the drumming rituals of Siberia, the visionary practices of Native American cultures, or the plant medicine ceremonies of South America, shamanism offers a wealth of wisdom and healing. So, as you explore these practices, remember to honor their cultural roots and approach them with respect and humility.

4.2 ETHICAL CONSIDERATIONS IN SHAMANIC PRACTICE

Imagine you're at a shamanic gathering, the air thick with the scent of sage, the rhythmic beat of drums echoing in your chest. Amidst the spiritual enthusiasm, it's easy to get caught up in the moment and forget the importance of ethics in shamanic practice. However, ethical considerations are crucial for maintaining the integrity of shamanic work. Respect for cultural traditions and origins is paramount. Shamanism is deeply rooted in the artistic and spiritual practices of indigenous peoples. Misappropriating or diluting these practices can disrespect their origins and weaken the shamanic work's power and authenticity. Ethical responsibility in healing practices is also vital. As a shamanic practitioner, you hold a position of trust and power. Your actions can profoundly impact the well-being of those you work with. Maintaining high ethical standards ensures that your practice remains a force for good.

So, what are the ethical guidelines for practicing shamanism? First and foremost is the principle of doing no harm and respect for all beings. This means approaching your work with compassion and empathy, ensuring that your actions do not cause harm to others or the environment. Confidentiality and consent are also crucial. Just like in any healing practice, respecting the privacy of your clients is essential. Always seek explicit consent before initiating physical contact or energy exchange. This fosters trust and creates a safe space for healing. Integrity in teaching and sharing shamanic knowledge is another key principle. Avoid sensationalizing or commercializing shamanic practices. Instead, focus on sharing authentic, respectful knowledge that honors the traditions you are drawing from.

Ethical dilemmas can arise in shamanic practice, and it is important to navigate them carefully. One common issue is the use of plant medicine. While these powerful tools can offer profound healing, they also come with risks and ethical considerations. Before using plant medicine, please ensure you and your clients are fully informed about the potential effects and risks.

Respecting your client's privacy and autonomy is another potential dilemma. Maintaining strict confidentiality and ensuring your clients feel safe and respected throughout the healing process is essential.

Allow me to share some personal anecdotes and scenarios to illustrate these points. One case involved a client who sought my help with a deeply personal issue. She was hesitant to share details, fearing judgment. I assured her that everything discussed would remain confidential and sought her consent before proceeding with any healing work. This created a safe space for her to open up, leading to a successful healing session. Another scenario involved a group ceremony where plant medicine was used. I provided detailed information about the effects and potential risks, ensuring that all participants gave informed consent. This fostered trust and ensured that everyone had a positive and safe experience.

Navigating ethical boundaries can be challenging, but it's crucial for maintaining the integrity of shamanic practice. One personal story that stands out involved a client going through a difficult time and seeking frequent sessions. While I wanted to help, I recognized the importance of not creating dependency. I encouraged her to integrate the insights from our sessions into her daily life, empowering her to take charge of her healing journey. This approach respected her autonomy and prevented unhealthy dependency on the shamanic work.

Ethical considerations in shamanic practice are not just about following rules but about fostering a respectful, compassionate, and authentic connection with shamanism's spiritual and cultural roots. By adhering to principles of non-harm, confidentiality, consent, and integrity, you can ensure that your practice remains a force for good. Whether working with plant medicine, conducting healing sessions, or sharing shamanic knowledge, always approach your work with respect and empathy. This honors the traditions you are drawing from and ensures that your practice remains a powerful and authentic path to healing and spiritual growth.

4.3 RESPECTING INDIGENOUS TRADITIONS

Imagine you're attending a ceremony led by an indigenous shaman. The air is filled with the scent of burning sage, and the rhythmic beat of drums resonates deeply within you. This isn't a spectacle; it's a sacred tradition passed down through genera-tions. Respecting indigenous shamanic traditions is crucial in honoring and preserving their cultural heritage. Indigenous knowledge forms the bedrock of shamanism, offering wisdom that has stood the test of time. However, colonization's impact has been devastating, often eroding these rich traditions. Colonization brought physical conquest and cultural suppression, losing languages, rituals, and spiritual practices.

To engage respectfully with indigenous traditions, seek permis-sion and guidance from indigenous practitioners. This isn't about asking for a tourist map; it's about building relationships based on mutual respect and understanding. Support indigenous communities and initiatives by attending workshops, contributing to community projects, or buying their crafts. These actions not only show respect but also help sustain their cultural practices. Cultural humility is essential. Approach these traditions with an open heart and a willingness to learn. Acknowledge your own cultural biases and be prepared to set them aside. This humility allows for a genuine connection and a deeper understanding of the practices.

Understanding one's own cultural biases is a crucial step in this journey. We all carry preconceived notions shaped by our upbringing and society. Recognizing these biases helps you approach indigenous traditions with a fresh perspective. Imagine you're a blank slate, ready to absorb new teachings without judgment. This openness is about intellectual understanding and emotional and spiritual receptivity. Indigenous shamans often stress the importance of approaching their traditions with respect and humility. One shaman I spoke with, who prefers to remain anonymous, shared a story about a non-indigenous practitioner who came to learn but ended up teaching instead. The shaman gently reminded them that authentic learning begins with the art of listening.

Quotes and stories from indigenous shamans offer invaluable insights. For instance, a Nemenhah elder once told me, "Our ways are not just rituals; they are a way of life." This statement encapsulates the depth and significance of indigenous shamanic practices. These traditions are not mere performances but deeply ingrained aspects of their culture and spirituality. Successful collaborations with indigenous communities often involve a reciprocal exchange of knowledge and support. One example is a project in the Amazon where local shamans collaborated with researchers to document their plant medicine knowledge. This partnership not only preserved valuable information but also provided resources for the community.

Respecting indigenous traditions is not just about following rules but building meaningful relationships. Approaching these traditions with respect, humility, and an open heart contributes to preserving and honoring the rich cultural heritage of indigenous shamanic practices. So, next time you find yourself in the presence of an indigenous shaman, remember that you are not just a participant; you are a custodian of ancient wisdom.

4.4 THE IMPORTANCE OF CULTURAL AUTHENTICITY

Cultural authenticity in shamanic practice is like the secret ingredient in a family recipe. It's the essence that makes the practice truly meaningful and effective. Authenticity means staying true to the roots and traditions from which shamanism originates. It's about honoring the original practices, beliefs, and tools passed down through generations. Authenticity is a key principle in shamanic practice because it ensures that the rituals and ceremonies retain their intended power and significance. Without it, shamanism risks becoming diluted, losing its depth and efficacy. Misrepresenting these traditions can lead to practices that are shallow at best and harmful at worst, stripping away the very essence that makes shamanism a profound spiritual path.

So, how do you ensure cultural authenticity in your shamanic practice? One of the most effective ways is to learn directly from traditional practitioners. Seek out indigenous shamans or experienced practitioners trained in the authentic ways of shamanism. Attend workshops, read books, and participate in ceremonies led by these practitioners. This firsthand experience provides invaluable insights and helps you understand the deeper nuances of the practice. Using traditional tools and methods is another crucial step. Whether it's a specific type of drum, a particular herb for smudging, or a traditional chant, using these authentic elements helps maintain the integrity of your practice.

The impact of Westernization on shamanic practices cannot be ignored. Western interpretations often simplify and commercialize these ancient traditions, focusing more on marketability than authenticity. The influence of New Age movements has led to a version of shamanism that sometimes resembles a spiritual buffet, picking and choosing elements without understanding their cultural context. While modern adaptations can make shamanism more accessible, balancing these with traditional authenticity is crucial. This means not just borrowing rituals because they are trendy but understanding and respecting their origins and significance.

Consider the story of a friend who traveled to Siberia to learn from a traditional shaman. She participated in ceremonies involving specific drumming rhythms and chants, which invoke spirits and facilitate healing. Upon returning, she incorporated these authentic practices into her work, maintaining their integrity and power. Another example is a practitioner who uses traditional Amazonian plant medicine ceremonies. By learning directly from indigenous shamans and following their precise methods, he ensures his practice remains true to its roots, providing genuine healing and spiritual insights.

Authentic healing ceremonies from various cultures offer profound examples of cultural authenticity. In Mongolia, shamans perform healing rituals involving drumming, singing, and using sacred objects like mirrors and swords. These ceremonies are deeply rooted in Mongolian culture and spirituality, retaining their original power and significance. In Africa, sangomas conduct healing ceremonies using drumming, dancing, and herbal medicine, following traditions passed down for generations. These authentic practices provide effective healing and spiritual guidance, demonstrating the importance of cultural authenticity in shamanism.

Personal stories of practicing authentic shamanism highlight the transformative power of staying true to traditional methods. One practitioner shared how a traditional Nemenhah Itsipi (sweat lodge ceremony) helped her release deep-seated emotional pain and gain clarity in her life. By following the authentic practices taught by Native shaman elders, she experienced a profound healing that wouldn't have been possible with a diluted version of the ceremony. Another practitioner described how participating in an authentic Ayahuasca ceremony led by A Peruvian shaman provided insights and healing that transformed his approach to life.

Maintaining cultural authenticity in shamanic practice is not just about following rules. It's about honoring the wisdom and traditions of the cultures from which shamanism originates. By learning directly from traditional practitioners, using authentic tools and methods, and balancing modern adaptations with traditional practices, you can ensure that your shamanic work remains powerful and meaningful. Authenticity brings depth and efficacy to shamanism, allowing you to experience its true transformative power.

4.5 LEARNING FROM INDIGENOUS SHAMANS: INTERVIEWS AND INSIGHTS

My first introduction to the shaman's path was from my father, Genaro Garcia Von-Lembcke; he would take me to his lectures as a young boy; little did I know then that I was on the path to a life-changing way to see, explore, and experience the world and all its beauty and abundance it has for us all. My father would tell me to Imagine sitting with a master chef to learn their secret recipes. Now, replace the kitchen with a sacred circle and the chef with a Peruvian Chaman (shaman). Learning directly from indigenous shamans is invaluable. He would say our ancestors would carry the wisdom, offering insights beyond textbooks and seminars, most of which were from oral tradition and teachings. They provide a depth of understanding that ensures the practice remains authentic and respectful. Gaining deeper insights, experience, and understanding from these traditional keepers of shamanic knowledge can profoundly enrich your journey. This would ensure the authenticity of the practice becomes much easier when one learns from those who have lived and breathed these traditions, like our family, for generations.

I had the privilege of interviewing White Eagle, a medicine woman who shared fascinating insights into traditional healing methods. White Eagle described the intricate rituals involving drumming, chanting, and using sacred objects during the drum ceremony. These items aren't just tools but extensions of the shaman's spiritual energy. White Eagle emphasized the importance of intention and respect in every ritual. She explained that with these elements, the rituals would retain their potency. She also shared stories of the drum healing ceremonies where the spirits of ancestors played crucial roles in guiding the process and providing wisdom.

Another enlightening conversation was with a Nemenhah Shaman, Chief Cloudpiler. Chief Cloudpiler spoke about the deep connection between the land and their spiritual practices. He described how every plant, animal, and even rock has its spirit and how these spirits are integral to their healing rituals. One of his most memorable teachings was about the Vision Quest, a rite of passage where individuals seek solitude in nature to gain insights and guidance. Chief Cloudpiler emphasized that this quest is not just about seeking answers but about forming a relationship with the natural world and understanding one's place.

I also had the opportunity to learn from Peruvian Master Shaman Juan Oscoa and later from his teacher, Yankunta, and his nephew, Jairo Osco. Yankunta's teachings revolved around the use of Ayahuasca, a sacred plant medicine used for deep spiritual healing and insight. He explained that the plant is a teacher, guiding participants through visions and emotional releases. Yankunta stressed the importance of preparation and integration, noting that the true work begins after the ceremony. He shared stories of individuals who found profound healing through Ayahuasca, not just from physical ailments but from deep-seated emotional traumas.

Several key lessons emerged from these interviews. Respect and humility were common themes across all teachings. Each shaman emphasized the importance of approaching the practice with a humble heart and a respectful mind. They also highlighted the unique teachings from their cultural perspectives. White Eagle spoke of the power of ancestral spirits, Chief Cloudpiler of the intimate relationship with the land through permaculture, Jairo of the connection with Pachamama and her fauna and flora, and Yankunta of the wisdom of plant spirits and the connection to the universe. These varied perspectives enrich the understanding of shamanism, offering a multifaceted approach to spiritual and healing practices.

Incorporating these insights into your practice involves practical applications of indigenous wisdom. For instance, you might integrate the use of sacred objects, as Chief Cloudpiler mentioned, ensuring they are used with respect and intention. You could also adopt the practice of forming a relationship with nature, as Chief Cloudpiler teaches, by spending time in solitude and listening to the spirits of the land. If you choose to work with plant medicine, follow Yankunta's advice on thorough preparation and integration, treating the plant as a revered teacher.

Creating a respectful and authentic shamanic practice means honoring the teachings of these indigenous shamans. This involves adopting their practices and understanding the cultural and spiritual contexts from which they arise. Approach your practice with sincerity, always seeking to learn and grow. Remember, shamanism is not just a set of rituals; it's a way of life deeply connected to the world around you. Integrating these lessons ensures your practice remains true to its roots, offering genuine healing and spiritual growth.

4.6 AVOIDING CULTURAL APPROPRIATION IN SHAMANIC WORK

Imagine strolling through a bustling market where vendors sell dreamcatchers, smudge sticks, and shamanic drums. While these items might seem like charming souvenirs, they often represent a deeper issue: cultural appropriation. Cultural appropriation occurs when elements of one culture, frequently a marginalized or indigenous group, are taken and used by another culture, usually without permission or understanding. This practice can strip sacred traditions of their meaning and disrespect the cultures they originate from. In shamanism, this is particularly harmful. Indigenous communities often face the commercialization of their sacred practices, leading to a loss of cultural significance and exploitation.

To avoid cultural appropriation in your shamanic practice, it's crucial to understand and respect cultural boundaries. This means recognizing that not all practices are open to everyone. Some ceremonies, rituals, and tools are sacred and reserved for those within the culture. Seek permission and guidance from indigenous practitioners when exploring these practices. This isn't just about asking for a green light; it's about understanding these practices' context, significance, and proper use. Avoid commercializing sacred practices. Selling or profiting from these traditions without giving back to the communities they come from is exploitative. Support indigenous artists and practitioners by purchasing goods directly and contributing to community initiatives.

Cultural sensitivity is about being aware and respectful of the cultural context in which shamanic practices exist. Recognize and address your own cultural biases. We all carry preconceived notions shaped by our backgrounds. Acknowledging these biases allows you to approach shamanic practices with a fresh perspective. Practicing with cultural awareness and respect means doing your homework. You can learn about the cultures you are engaging with, their history, and their current challenges. This knowledge fosters a more respectful and informed practice.

Let's explore examples to illustrate the difference between respectful and disrespectful practices. Consider a case where a non-indigenous practitioner sought to lead an Ayahuasca ceremony. Instead of diving in headfirst, he spent years learning from Peruvian shamans, gaining their trust and permission. He ensured that his practice honored the traditions and contributed to the community. This respectful engagement fostered mutual respect and understanding. On the flip side, there are numerous instances of cultural appropriation. Take the example of a wellness brand that started selling "shamanic smudge kits" without any understanding of their cultural significance. Indigenous communities criticized the brand for taking their sacred rituals and making them into their commodity, stripping them of their spiritual meaning. This disrespectful practice led to backlash and calls for accountability.

The impact of cultural appropriation on indigenous communities is profound. It often leads to the breakdown of cultural significance and the exploitation of sacred practices. When these traditions are commercialized or misrepresented, they lose their depth and meaning. Indigenous communities, already struggling with the effects of colonization, face further marginalization when their sacred practices are treated as trends. The consequences aren't just cultural; they are deeply personal and spiritual, affecting the very fabric of these communities.

Avoiding cultural appropriation isn't just about following rules; it's about fostering a genuine, respectful relationship with the cultures you engage with. By understanding and respecting cultural boundaries, seeking permission and guidance, and practicing with cultural sensitivity, you can ensure that your shamanic work honors the traditions it draws from. This not only enriches your practice but also contributes to the preservation and respect of indigenous cultures. So, the next time you find yourself drawn to a shamanic practice, take a moment to consider its origins and approach it with the respect and understanding it deserves.

In this chapter, we've explored the importance of cultural context and authenticity in shamanic practices. From understanding the history and ethical considerations to respecting indigenous traditions and avoiding cultural appropriation, these elements form the foundation of a respectful and authentic shamanic practice. As we move forward, we'll delve into the transformative power of shamanism, exploring how these ancient practices can bring profound healing and growth in our modern lives.

MAKE A DIFFERENCE WITH YOUR REVIEW

"The best way to find yourself is to lose yourself in the service of others."

MAHATMA GANDHI

As you explore *The Shaman's Path for Beginners*, I hope you're starting to feel more confident in your journey toward holistic health. I'd like to ask for a small favor that could make a big difference.

Would you help someone like you who is curious about shamanism but needs help figuring out where to start?

I aim to make learning about shamanic practices easy and fun for everyone. But to reach more people, I need your help.

Most people choose books based on reviews. By sharing your thoughts, you could guide someone ready to explore but unsure of where to begin. It costs nothing and takes less than a minute, but your review could change someone's path. Your words could help...

...one more person finds healing and balance.

...one more beginner discovers the power of shamanic practices.

...one more reader unlocks their inner strength.

To make a difference, simply scan the QR code below and leave a review:

If you love helping others, thank you so much from the bottom of my heart!

—Iggy Garcia

CHAPTER 5
INTEGRATING SHAMANISM INTO DAILY LIFE

You know, shamanism isn't just for those quiet, misty forests or ancient ceremonial grounds. Imagine trying to bring a bit of that mystical charm into your bustling, modern life. Picture yourself sipping your morning coffee, perhaps not in a sacred grove but in your kitchen, yet still finding a moment of profound spiritual connection. The beauty of shamanism is its adaptability; it can fit into your daily routine as seamlessly as your favorite pair of slippers.

5.1 DAILY RITUALS FOR SPIRITUAL CONNECTION

Let's talk about daily rituals. You might think, "Rituals? Isn't that reserved for full moons and special occasions?" Not quite. Daily rituals are the unsung heroes of a consistent spiritual practice. They provide a steady rhythm that keeps you connected to your spiritual path, much like brushing your teeth, which keeps you connected to your dentist's good graces. The significance of daily commitment lies in its ability to ground you, offering a sense of stability amid the chaos of modern life. Creating a routine that fits into your everyday schedule ensures that spirituality becomes an integral, rather than an occasional, part of your life.

Consider starting your day with a simple morning gratitude practice. As soon as you wake up, before diving into the whirlwind of emails and breakfast prep, take a moment to reflect on three things you're grateful for. They don't have to be grandiose; even appreciation for a good night's sleep or a sunny day works wonders. This practice sets a positive tone for the day and opens your heart to the blessings around you. In the evening, try a reflection and intention-setting ritual. As you wind down, think about your day. What went well? What could have been better? Set an intention for the next day, something you want to focus on or achieve. This practice brings closure to your day and prepares your subconscious for the night ahead.

Another simple yet powerful daily ritual is smudging or energy cleansing. Use sage, palo santo, or your preferred cleansing tool to clear your energy field and living space. Light the smudge stick, let the smoke move around you, and visualize any negative energy dissipating. This practice purifies your environment and refreshes your mind and spirit, allowing positive energy to flow.

The benefits of these daily rituals are manifold. Firstly, they increase your sense of peace and grounding. There's something profoundly comforting about starting and ending your day with a moment of spiritual connection. It's like a mental and emotional reset button. Secondly, these practices strengthen your connection with spirit guides. Regularly tuning in creates a channel for ongoing communication and guidance. Lastly, daily rituals enhance mindfulness and presence. They pull you out of autopilot mode, making you more aware of the present moment and your inner state.

Maintaining consistency with daily rituals can be challenging, especially with a busy schedule. But it's not impossible. One practical tip is to set reminders. Use your phone's alarm or a calendar app to remind you of your morning and evening rituals. Creating a dedicated ritual space can also help. It doesn't have to be elaborate—a small corner with candles, crystals, or meaningful objects will do. This space serves as a visual cue and a sacred environment where you can perform your rituals without distraction.

Integrating rituals into existing routines is another effective strategy. Combine your morning gratitude practice with your first cup of coffee or tea. Reflect on your day and set intentions while brushing your teeth before bed. These minor adjustments make it easier to stick to your rituals without feeling like they're an additional chore. The idea is to weave spirituality into the fabric of your daily life, making it as natural and effortless as possible.

Reflection Exercise: Crafting Your Daily Rituals

Take a few minutes to think about what daily rituals could fit into your life. Consider your morning and evening routines. What small, meaningful practices can you incorporate? Write down your ideas and try them out for a week. Observe how these rituals affect your mood, energy, and spiritual connection. Adjust as needed to find what works best for you.

Daily rituals are the backbone of a consistent spiritual practice. They ground you, connect you with your spirit guides, and enhance your mindfulness. By starting small and integrating these practices into your existing routines, you can cultivate a daily spiritual practice that enriches your life and keeps you connected to your shamanic path. So, light that sage, count your blessings, and set your intentions. Your spiritual journey is about to become much more grounded and meaningful.

5.2 BUILDING A DEEPER CONNECTION WITH NATURE

Shamanism and nature go together like peanut butter and jelly. Connecting with nature isn't just a quaint pastime; it's a fundamental aspect of shamanic practice. Nature serves as both a teacher and a healer. Imagine a wise, old sage who's seen it all, offering your patience, resilience, and interconnectedness lessons. That's the nature of shamanism. The natural world provides a classroom where every tree, river, and rock carries wisdom. During shamanic journeys and rituals, nature acts as a backdrop and a participant, enhancing the spiritual experience. The rustling leaves, flowing water, and chirping birds aren't just ambient sounds; they're part of the symphony that guides you.

To deepen your relationship with nature, consider mindful nature walks and meditations. Next time you're out for a walk, slow down and engage all your senses. Feel the earth beneath your feet, hear the wind rustling through the leaves, and smell the fresh air. This isn't just a stroll; it's a conversation with the natural world. Another technique is creating a nature altar or sacred garden. Find a spot in your yard or even a windowsill where you can place natural items like stones, feathers, and plants. This space becomes a mini sanctuary, a place to connect with nature's energy daily. Practicing eco-shamanism involves rituals that honor the Earth. Simple acts like prayer before planting a tree or thanking the elements for their support can make a big difference. These rituals honor nature and remind you of your role as a caretaker of the Earth Mother.

Seasonal and environmental awareness is another crucial aspect. Aligning shamanic practices with the changing seasons and local environment enhances their effectiveness. Seasonal rituals and ceremonies, like celebrating the solstices and equinoxes, help you attune to nature's rhythms. Use local plants and natural materials in your rituals to strengthen your connection to your specific environment. Imagine celebrating the arrival of spring by incorporating blooming flowers and fresh herbs from your garden into your rituals. This practice not only grounds you in the present but also connects you to the cycles of nature.

Let me share a personal story to illustrate the transformative power of nature connection. A few years ago, I decided to spend a weekend camping alone in the woods. One evening, as I sat by the campfire, a gentle breeze rustled the leaves, creating a soothing melody. I closed my eyes and tuned into the sounds around me. Suddenly, I felt an overwhelming sense of peace and oneness with the world. It was as if the trees, the wind, and the fire communicated with me, sharing their ancient wisdom. That experience profoundly deepened my connection to nature and enriched my shamanic practice.

Another practitioner I know shared a transformative experience during a nature-based shamanic ritual. She had been feeling lost and disconnected for months. She decided to perform a water blessing ritual at a nearby river. Standing by the water, she offered her prayers and intentions, asking for clarity and guidance. As she finished, a Great Blue Heron appeared on the opposite bank, standing still and graceful. The sight of the heron brought her a sense of calm and reassurance. She interpreted the heron's presence as a sign that she was on the right path. This experience gave her the clarity she sought and strengthened her bond with nature.

Connecting with nature is more than a feel-good activity; it's vital to shamanic practice. You can deepen your relationship with the natural world by engaging in mindful nature walks, creating sacred spaces, and practicing eco-shamanism. Aligning your practices with the changing seasons and local environment further enhances this connection. Whether through personal experiences or rituals, nature offers profound wisdom and healing that can transform your spiritual journey. So, go ahead, step outside, and let nature be your guide. The trees, the wind, and the water are waiting to share their secrets with you.

5.3 SHAMANIC PRACTICES FOR STRESS RELIEF

Stress is like that uninvited guest who overstays their welcome, affecting your mind, body, and spirit. It sneaks in, making your muscles tense, your mind restless, and your spirit weary. But here's the good news: shamanic practices can help you manage and reduce this unwelcome visitor. The impact of stress on your overall well-being is profound, causing everything from headaches and fatigue to anxiety and depression. Shamanism's holistic approach can promote relaxation and balance, helping you find your center amidst the chaos.

Imagine sitting quietly, your eyes closed, focusing on your breath. This simple act of breathwork can be incredibly grounding. Begin by inhaling deeply through your nose, letting your belly rise, and then exhaling slowly through your mouth. As you breathe, visualize roots growing from your feet into the Earth, anchoring you firmly. This grounding exercise helps you feel stable and connected, reducing the jittery effects of stress. Another effective technique is drumming or rattling. The rhythmic beat of a drum or the shake of a rattle can transport you to a calmer state of mind. Sit comfortably, close your eyes, and let the sound wash over you. Feel the vibrations releasing tension from your body, leaving you more relaxed and at peace.

Visualization and guided imagery are also powerful stress-relief tools. Picture yourself in a serene place, like a tranquil forest or a peaceful beach. Engage all your senses—feel the sand beneath your feet, hear the gentle waves, smell the salty air. This mental escape can provide a much-needed break from the pressures of daily life, giving your mind and body a chance to relax. Guided imagery can be even more effective when combined with shamanic elements. Imagine a spirit guide or power animal joining you in this serene setting, offering comfort and guidance. Their presence can amplify the calming effects, helping you feel more supported and less alone.

The benefits of these shamanic stress-relief practices are numerous. They can enhance relaxation and calmness, making it easier to navigate daily challenges with a clear and focused mind. Better emotional regulation and resilience are other positive outcomes. Regularly engaging in these practices can build a buffer against stress, making it easier to bounce back from setbacks. The most profound benefit is increased inner peace and stability. When stress rears its ugly head, you can tap into these practices to regain your equilibrium, feeling more grounded and centered.

Incorporating these stress-relief techniques into your daily life doesn't have to be a Herculean task. Short, daily practices can be surprisingly effective. Dedicate five to ten minutes daily to a grounding exercise, drumming session, or visualization. You can even combine these practices with other activities. For example, do a quick breathwork exercise while waiting for your morning coffee to brew, or take a few moments to visualize a peaceful scene before bed. Creating a stress-relief toolkit can also be helpful. This toolkit might include a small drum or rattle, a candle, a calming essential oil, and a list of your favorite visualization exercises. Keep this toolkit in an easily accessible place, like your bedside table or office desk, so you can reach for it whenever you need a quick stress-buster.

Another practical tip is to set aside specific times during the day for these practices. Starting your day with a grounding exercise sets a positive tone, while a short drumming session during lunch can provide a much-needed energy boost. In the evening, a visualization exercise can help you unwind and prepare for a restful night's sleep. The key is to find what works best for you and make it a routine. Consistency is crucial; the more you engage in these practices, the more effective they become at reducing stress and promoting overall well-being.

Incorporating shamanic practices into your life for stress relief can provide a holistic approach to managing the pressures of modern life. Breathwork, drumming, and visualization can enhance relaxation, emotional regulation, and inner peace. These practices offer a sanctuary, a place to retreat and find balance amidst the chaos. So, take a deep breath, close your eyes, and let the wisdom of shamanism guide you to a calmer, more centered state of being.

5.4 USING SHAMANIC TECHNIQUES FOR PERSONAL GROWTH

Shamanism offers a unique path to self-awareness and personal transformation. It's not just about connecting with the spirit world; it's also a profound journey into your psyche. Imagine it as a mirror reflecting aspects of yourself that you might not see otherwise. The practices and rituals of shamanism help you peel back the layers, revealing your true self. This process of self-discovery can be both enlightening and transformative, providing you with the tools to navigate life's challenges with greater clarity and purpose.

One powerful technique for personal growth in shamanism is the vision quest. This involves spending time in solitude, often in nature, to gain clarity and insight. Picture yourself in a secluded spot, free from the distractions of daily life. You might fast, meditate, or sit in silence, allowing the wisdom of the natural world to seep in. Vision quests help you find answers to pressing questions, better understand your path, and connect with your inner self. They can be intense but incredibly rewarding, offering profound insights that can guide your personal and spiritual journey.

Another method is working with spirit guides. These spiritual allies offer guidance and wisdom, helping you navigate the complexities of life. You can connect with them through meditation, rituals, or even during shamanic journeys. Imagine having a wise mentor who provides insights and support whenever needed. Spirit guides can help you set and achieve personal goals, providing clarity and motivation to move forward. They offer a unique perspective, often revealing solutions you might have yet to consider.

Rituals are also a powerful tool for personal growth. You can manifest your goals and desires by setting clear intentions and performing specific actions. For instance, you might create a ritual to release old habits or to invite new opportunities into your life. These rituals can be simple or elaborate, depending on your preference. The key is to perform them with intention and focus, aligning your actions with your goals. This helps you achieve your objectives and reinforces your commitment to personal growth.

Power animals, too, play a significant role in overcoming personal challenges. These spiritual allies embody specific qualities and strengths that you can draw upon. Imagine facing a problematic situation and calling upon a lion's courage or an owl's wisdom.

Power animals provide support and guidance, helping you navigate obstacles more easily. They remind you of your strengths and capabilities, empowering you to face challenges head-on.

The benefits of these shamanic practices are profound. They can lead to a greater sense of purpose and direction, helping you understand your path and what you must do to stay on it. Enhanced self-awareness and intuition are other significant benefits. As you engage in these practices, you'll develop a deeper understanding of yourself and your surroundings, making it easier to navigate life's complexities. Empowerment and confidence in your abilities are the most transformative benefits. By connecting with your inner strengths and wisdom, you'll feel more capable and confident, ready to take on whatever comes your way.

Consider, for example, the story of Lisa, a woman who felt stuck in her career and personal life. She decided to undertake a vision quest, spending three days in solitude in the mountains. She gained profound insights into her passions and needed changes during this time. Upon returning, she felt a renewed sense of purpose and clarity, eventually transitioning to a career aligned with her passions. Her journey was transformative, giving her the direction and motivation to change significantly.

Another example is John, who struggled with self-doubt and anxiety. Through regular meditation and connection with his spirit guides, he gained the confidence to pursue his goals. His spirit guides provided the support and encouragement he needed, helping him overcome his fears and take bold steps in his personal and professional life. John's experience highlights the transformative power of shamanic practices, showing how they can lead to significant personal growth and fulfillment.

Shamanism offers a rich tapestry of practices and techniques supporting personal growth and self-discovery. Whether through vision quests, working with spirit guides, performing rituals, or connecting with power animals, these practices provide valuable tools for navigating life's challenges and achieving your goals. The profound benefits lead to greater self-awareness, empowerment, and a more profound sense of purpose. So, take the plunge, explore these practices, and watch them transform your life in ways you never imagined.

5.5 ENHANCING YOUR INTUITION WITH SHAMANIC PRACTICES

Intuition in shamanism is like having a spiritual GPS that guides you through the complexities of life. It's not just a hunch or a gut feeling; it's a finely tuned spiritual tool. Intuition plays a crucial role in shamanic practices, helping you navigate the realms of spirit and healing with confidence and clarity. Whether seeking guidance during a shamanic journey, making important life decisions, or performing healing work, intuition acts as your inner compass, pointing you in the right direction.

To enhance your intuition, start with meditation and mindfulness practices. These foundational techniques help quiet the mind and create space for intuitive insights to emerge. Find a quiet spot, sit comfortably, and focus on your breath. Pay attention to subtle impressions or feelings that arise as your mind settles. These are often the whispers of your intuition. Working with spirit guides can also amplify your intuitive abilities. Ask your spirit guides to help develop your intuition during meditation or shamanic journeys. They can provide insights and symbols that enhance your intuitive awareness.

Journaling and dreamwork are other effective methods for cultivating intuition. Please keep a journal by your bedside and jot down your dreams or impressions when you wake. Dreams are a rich source of intuitive insights, often revealing messages from your subconscious mind or spirit guides. Reflecting on these entries can help you identify patterns and deepen your intuitive understanding. Using divination tools like oracle cards or pendulums can also provide valuable guidance. Draw a card or use a pendulum to ask specific questions, and trust the answers you receive. These tools bridge your conscious mind and the intuitive realm, offering clarity and direction.

A strong intuition offers numerous benefits. It provides greater clarity and confidence in your choices, making it easier to navigate life's challenges. Imagine facing a difficult decision and feeling a robust, intuitive sense of the right path. This inner knowing can save you time and reduce stress. Enhanced intuition also strengthens your connection with spiritual guidance. By tuning into your intuitive abilities, you create direct communication with your spirit guides, receiving their wisdom and support more readily. This connection can provide comfort and guidance, especially during difficult times.

I'd like to share a personal anecdote to show the power of intuition. A few years ago, I was considering a significant career change. I felt torn between staying in my current coaching position and pursuing a new opportunity that seemed risky but exciting. During a meditation session, I asked my spirit guides for guidance. I received a vivid image of a path diverging in a forest, with one direction bathed in sunlight and the other shrouded in shadows. This intuitive vision gave me the clarity I needed to choose the brighter path, leading me to stay in my current position and develop and change things that would align me with new ideas and passion in my current coaching position.

Another example involves a friend who relied on her intuition to navigate a challenging personal situation. She had been experiencing recurring dreams about a specific symbol—a white feather. Intrigued, she began journaling her dreams and meditating on the feather's meaning. Over time, she realized the feather symbolized a need for peace and clarity. This intuitive insight prompted her to make changes that brought greater harmony and balance, improving her overall well-being.

Developing and trusting your intuition can be a transformative experience. It enhances decision-making, strengthens spiritual connections, and helps you navigate life's complexities more easily. You can cultivate a strong, reliable intuition by incorporating meditation, working with spirit guides, journaling, and using divination tools. This inner guidance system offers invaluable support, helping you make choices that align with your highest good and spiritual path. So, take a moment to tune in, listen to those subtle whispers, and let your intuition guide you to a more empowered and fulfilling life.

5.6 SHAMANIC PRACTICES FOR EMOTIONAL HEALING

Emotional healing is one of the most profound gifts that shamanism offers. Think of it as a holistic approach to emotional well-being, addressing not just the symptoms but the root causes of emotional pain and trauma. Unlike conventional methods focusing solely on the mind or body, shamanic practices integrate the spiritual dimension, providing a more comprehensive healing experience. Emotional wounds, whether from recent events or long-buried traumas, can significantly impact one's overall well-being. Addressing these wounds through spiritual practices is crucial for achieving a balanced and harmonious life.

Soul retrieval is one of the most potent techniques for emotional healing in shamanism. Imagine feeling fragmented, as if pieces of your soul are scattered across time and space. Soul retrieval involves journeying into the spiritual realm to reclaim these lost parts, restoring your sense of wholeness. This practice is particularly effective for healing emotional trauma, as it targets the core of your being. Reintegrating these lost fragments can heal deep-seated emotional wounds, leading to a more complete and balanced self.

Energy work is another powerful method for releasing negative emotions. Picture your energy field as a river; you feel vibrant and alive when it flows freely. However, emotional pain can create blockages, causing stagnation. Techniques such as smudging, using crystals, or visualizing a cleansing light can help remove these blockages, allowing your energy to flow freely again. This not only alleviates emotional pain but also revitalizes your entire being.

Rituals for forgiveness and letting go are essential for emotional healing. Holding on to grudges or past hurts can weigh you down, affecting your mental and emotional health. Create a simple ritual where you write down what you need to release on paper. Burn the paper in a safe container, visualizing the smoke carrying away your burdens. This symbolic act can provide a sense of closure and emotional freedom, allowing positive energy to enter your life.

Working with power animals can offer emotional support. These spiritual allies embody qualities that can help you navigate emotional challenges. For instance, a lion can lend you courage as a powerful animal when dealing with fear. If you're struggling with sadness, a dolphin might bring joy and playfulness back into your life. Connecting with these power animals through meditation or journeying allows you to draw upon their strengths to support your emotional healing process.

The benefits of shamanic emotional healing practices are far-reaching. Increased emotional stability and resilience are some of the most immediate effects. By addressing the root causes of emotional pain, you build a stronger foundation for emotional health. A greater sense of inner peace and wholeness is another significant benefit. Navigating life's ups and downs is easier when you feel complete and balanced. The most practical benefit is the enhanced ability to cope with life's challenges. With a toolkit of shamanic practices, you're better equipped to handle stress, setbacks, and emotional turmoil.

Take, for example, the story of Maria, who had been struggling with grief after the loss of a loved one. Traditional therapy provided some relief, but she still felt a deep emptiness. She decided to try soul retrieval. During the session, she reconnected with a part of herself that had been lost in the grief. The experience was transformative, bringing her a sense of peace and wholeness that she hadn't felt in years. Another case is John, who has been dealing with chronic anger issues. Through energy work and rituals for letting go, he could release the pent-up anger, replacing it with a sense of calm and balance. His relationships improved, and he felt more at peace with himself.

Shamanic practices offer a unique and holistic approach to emotional healing. By integrating techniques such as soul retrieval, energy work, rituals, and working with power animals, you can address emotional pain at its root, leading to profound healing and transformation. These practices provide the tools for emotional balance, resilience, and well-being.

In the next chapter, we will explore how to cultivate a supportive shamanic community and the importance of ethical leadership in shamanic practice. Together, these elements create a nurturing environment for personal and collective growth, enriching your spiritual journey and enhancing your experience of shamanism.

ADVANCED SHAMANIC PRACTICES

6.1 VISION QUESTS: SEEKING SPIRITUAL INSIGHTS IN NATURE

Have you ever found yourself staring at your smartphone, wondering if there's more to life than endless notifications? Imagine ditching the digital noise and heading into the wild for a vision quest. It's like hitting the spiritual reset button. A vision quest is a profound shamanic practice seeking spiritual guidance and clarity. It involves time alone in nature, deeply connecting with yourself and the world. This ancient rite of passage helps you strip away the layers of daily distractions, allowing you to tune into your inner voice and the wisdom of the natural world. One of the most profound events in my life was when I requested a vision quest from my mentor, Chief Cloudpiler.

Preparing for a vision quest requires thoughtful planning. First, choose a meaningful location in nature. Whether it's a remote forest, a serene mountain, or a quiet beach, the place should resonate with you and provide a sense of solitude and connection. Next, set clear intentions for your quest. Ask yourself what you hope to gain—clarity on a life decision, healing, or perhaps a deeper spiritual connection. Write down your intentions to keep them focused during your time in nature. Fasting and cleansing rituals are also traditional preparatory steps. Fasting helps purify your body and mind, making you more receptive to spiritual insights. A cleansing ritual, such as smudging with sage, can clear any lingering negative energy and set the stage for your quest.

Once you're prepared, it's time to embark on your vision quest. Begin by entering a meditative state in nature. Find a comfortable spot to sit or lie down, close your eyes, and take several deep breaths. Allow the sounds, smells, and sensations of nature to envelop you. Stay attuned to signs and messages from the natural world. You might notice an animal approaching, a particular tree standing out, or even a shift in the weather. These are not mere coincidences; they are often messages from the spirit world. Techniques for enduring physical and mental challenges are essential during a vision quest. Nature can be unpredictable, and solitude can bring up a range of emotions. Practice grounding to maintain stability by visualizing roots growing from your feet into the earth. If you feel overwhelmed, focus on your breath and bring your attention back to your intentions.

Integrating the insights gained from your vision quest is as important as the quest itself. Upon returning, take time to journal and reflect on your experience. Write down any visions, messages, or emotions that arose during your time in nature. This helps solidify the insights and provides a record you can revisit.

Practical steps to incorporate these insights into your daily life are crucial. If your vision quest reveals a need for more self-care, create a plan to integrate self-care practices into your routine. If it offered clarity on a life decision, take actionable steps towards making that decision. Sharing the experience with a mentor or community can also be beneficial. Discussing your insights with someone who understands shamanic practices can provide additional perspectives and support.

Reflection Exercise: Integrating Vision Quest Insights

1. **Journal Your Experience:** Write down the details of your vision quest, including any significant visions, messages, or emotions.
2. **Reflect on the Insights:** Identify key themes or messages that emerged during your quest.
3. **Create an Action Plan:** Develop practical steps to incorporate these insights into your daily life.
4. **Share with a Mentor or Community:** Discuss your experience with a trusted mentor or shamanic community for additional support and guidance.

Engaging in a vision quest is a transformative experience that opens the door to deeper spiritual insights and personal growth. By preparing thoroughly, staying attuned to nature, and integrating the insights gained, you can navigate your life with greater clarity and purpose. So, pack your spiritual backpack, find your sacred spot in nature, and prepare for an adventure that could change your life.

6.2 DREAMWORK: INTERPRETING AND USING YOUR DREAMS

Picture this: you're deep in sleep, navigating a landscape that's as familiar as it is strange. Suddenly, a wise old owl lands on your shoulder, whispering profound and elusive secrets. In shamanic practice, dreams are seen as gateways to the subconscious and spiritual realms. They're not just random brain activity but messages from the spirit world. These nocturnal adventures can offer healing, guidance, and profound insights, making dream-work a vital aspect of shamanism.

The first step is improving dream recall to make the most of your dreams. Have you ever woken up with a foggy memory of an important dream? Keeping a dream journal by your bedside can help. As soon as you wake up, jot down everything you remember, no matter how trivial it seems. Over time, this practice can enhance your ability to recall dreams in detail. Another effective method is setting intentions before sleep. Before drifting off, tell yourself that you want to remember your dreams. It's like programming your subconscious to be on alert. Herbs and crystals can also aid in dream recall. Mugwort, an herb known for its dream-enhancing properties, can be placed under your pillow. Amethyst, a crystal associated with spiritual insight, can be kept nearby to enhance dream clarity.

Interpreting the symbols and messages in your dreams can feel like deciphering an ancient language. Common dream symbols often have universal meanings. For instance, water can represent emotions, while flying might symbolize freedom or aspiration. However, personalizing dream interpretation is crucial. A snake in one culture might signify danger, while in another, it represents transformation. Reflect on what specific symbols mean to you.

Consulting with spirit guides can also provide clarity. During meditation, ask your guides to help you understand the messages in your dreams. They might offer insights you hadn't considered, clarifying the dream's meaning.

Using dreams for spiritual growth is where dreamwork truly shines. Transforming dream insights into actionable steps can be incredibly empowering. How can you incorporate more self-care into your life if a dream reveals a need for more self-care? Maybe it's as simple as taking a walk in nature or setting aside time for meditation. Healing through dream re-entry techniques is another powerful tool. If a dream feels unresolved, you can re-enter it through meditation, asking for further guidance or healing. This technique allows you to continue the work started in the dream, bringing it to a more satisfying conclusion. Incorporating dreamwork into shamanic rituals can also amplify its impact. You might create a ritual to honor a significant dream, using symbols or objects from the dream to anchor the experience in your waking life.

Dreamwork Exercise: Enhancing Dream Recall

1. **Keep a Dream Journal:** Place it by your bedside. Write down your dreams as soon as you wake up.
2. **Set Intentions:** Before sleep, tell yourself you will remember your dreams.
3. **Use Dream Enhancers:** Place mug wort under your pillow or keep an amethyst crystal nearby.
4. **Reflect on Symbols:** Identify common symbols in your dreams and personalize their meanings.
5. **Consult Spirit Guides:** Ask for guidance in interpreting your dreams during meditation.

Dreams offer a rich tapestry of symbols and messages that can guide your spiritual path. By enhancing your dream recall, interpreting the symbols, and using the insights for personal growth, you can unlock the profound wisdom that lies within your subconscious. So, as you drift off to sleep tonight, remember that your dreams are more than just nighttime stories; they're windows to your soul and the spirit world.

6.3 THE MEDICINE WHEEL: BALANCING YOUR LIFE

Imagine a giant pie chart, but it represents your entire existence instead of showing your monthly expenses. Welcome to the medicine wheel, a symbolic and spiritual tool from many indigenous traditions worldwide. The medicine wheel embodies the circle of life, the four cardinal directions, and their corresponding elements, colors, and animal totems. It's like a spiritual Swiss Army knife designed to help you achieve balance and healing. Picture it as your GPS for navigating life's complexities, offering guidance on physical, emotional, mental, and spiritual levels.

Creating your medicine wheel is an enriching process that deepens your connection to nature and the spiritual world. First, select a serene location—perhaps a secluded corner of your backyard or a quiet forest clearing. The spot should be private and allow for contemplation and meditation. Gather natural materials such as stones, crystals, or twigs to represent the four directions: North, South, East, and West. Each direction has its own set of symbols, elements, and animal totems. For instance, the North is often associated with seeking wisdom from the spirit and the elements of earth and hummingbird, while the South represents passion, and fire looks within and the snake. Place your stones or markers in a circle, aligning them with these cardinal points. Once the physical arrangement is complete, consecrate the medicine wheel through a simple ritual. Light a candle or some incense, and pray or set an intention to bless the space. This act imbues the wheel with spiritual energy, making it a sacred space for your practices.

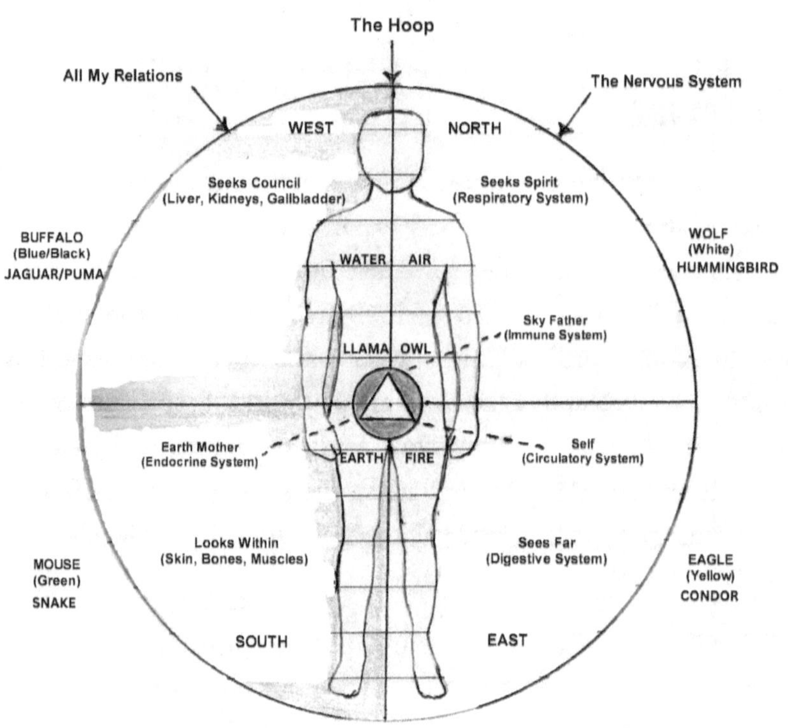

Using the medicine wheel for personal growth involves more than just admiring your handiwork. This tool can be a focal point for meditation, rituals, and ceremonies. Try meditating at different points of the wheel, focusing on the qualities and energies of each direction. For example, sit at the East point resented by air to see far and seek new beginnings and the condor, or at the West, water, seeking council from our ancestors, healing, jaguar or puma. Performing rituals at the medicine wheel can amplify their effectiveness. Whether you're conducting a full moon ceremony or a simple gratitude ritual, the wheel serves as a powerful anchor. Aligning with the energies of the four directions can provide a balanced approach to your spiritual practices, helping you draw on the specific qualities you need at any given time.

Balancing your life using the medicine wheel is akin to tuning a musical instrument. It helps ensure that all aspects of your being are in harmony. The wheel's structure encourages you to consider physical, emotional, mental, and spiritual balance. For instance, the North point (earth) can guide you in grounding, speaking your authentic voice, and addressing physical health practices, while the South point (fire) can inspire you to ignite your passions and creativity while working on core issues of self. Setting intentions and goals using the medicine wheel can be incredibly effective. Place a symbolic object or write down your goal and place it in the corresponding direction on the wheel. This act aligns your intentions with the natural and spiritual energies, increasing the likelihood of manifestation. Seasonal and cyclical awareness is another benefit. The wheel can help you stay in tune with the rhythms of nature, offering a framework for seasonal rituals and reflections.

Creating Your Medicine Wheel: A Step-by-Step Guide

1. **Choose a Suitable Location:**
   - Find a private, serene space for contemplation and meditation.
   - Consider areas with high energetic potential, such as spots where ley lines intersect.

2. **Gather Natural Materials:**
   - Collect stones, crystals, or twigs to represent the four directions.
   - Ensure the items resonate with you and your intentions.
3. **Place Stones or Markers:**
   - Arrange them in a circle, aligning with the cardinal directions (North, South, East, West).
   - Each direction should have its own set of symbols and elements.
4. **Consecrate the Medicine Wheel:**
   - Light a candle or incense, and pray or set an intention.
   - This act blesses the space, imbuing it with spiritual energy.

The medicine wheel is a versatile tool that offers a structured yet flexible approach to balancing your life. By creating your wheel, you establish a sacred space to guide you through personal growth, rituals, and achieving harmony in all aspects of your being. So, grab some stones, find your spot, and start building your spiritual GPS.

6.4 ADVANCED ENERGY HEALING TECHNIQUES

Have you ever felt like your energy is as tangled as a pair of old headphones? Advanced energy healing can untangle those knots and bring harmony back to your life. These techniques go beyond basic practices to address deeper energetic imbalances affecting your physical, emotional, and spiritual well-being. In shamanic practice, advanced energy healing is crucial for holistic healing, tackling issues that simple techniques might not resolve. Think of it as tuning a piano that has been out of sync for years; the results can be transformative.

One powerful method is sound healing with tuning forks and singing bowls. Imagine the soothing hum of a tuning fork resonating through your body, aligning your energy centers. Tuning forks produce specific frequencies that can penetrate deep into your energy field, clearing blockages and restoring balance. Singing bowls, on the other hand, create a harmonious vibration that can shift stagnant energy. To use these tools, start by striking the tuning fork or singing bowl and holding it close to the area where you feel a blockage. Allow the sound to permeate your body, visualizing the energy flowing smoothly again.

Advanced chakra balancing techniques are another essential aspect of energy healing. While you might be familiar with crucial chakra meditations, advanced techniques involve a more in-depth approach. Begin by lying down in a comfortable position. Visualize each chakra as a spinning wheel of light. Instead of focusing on their colors, imagine the energy flowing through each chakra, cleansing and balancing them. You can also use crystals corresponding to each chakra, placing them on your body to enhance healing. For instance, place an amethyst on your third eye chakra to boost intuition and spiritual insight.

Removing energetic blockages often requires a more hands-on approach. One technique involves using your hands to scan your energy field. Slowly move your hands a few inches above your body, paying attention to areas that feel dense or heavy. These sensations indicate blockages. To clear them, visualize a stream of light flowing from your hands into the blocked area, dissolving the stagnant energy. Another method is using breathwork. Take a deep breath, focusing on the blockage, and as you exhale, imagine the blockage being expelled from your body. Repeat this process until you feel the energy flowing freely.

Attuning to higher frequencies is vital for advanced healing. Higher frequencies can elevate your overall vibration, making it easier to maintain balance and well-being. Methods for raising your vibrational frequency include spending time in nature, practicing gratitude, and engaging in creative activities. Using crystals and sacred geometry can also enhance this process. Crystals like selenite and clear quartz are excellent for raising your vibration. Sacred geometry involves using shapes and patterns that resonate with higher frequencies. You might create a grid with crystals in a sacred geometric pattern, placing it in your meditation space to amplify the energy.

Case studies and personal experiences provide compelling evidence of the effectiveness of advanced energy healing. Take the example of Sarah, who struggled with chronic fatigue and emotional turmoil. Through a series of sessions involving tuning forks and chakra balancing, she experienced profound shifts. The sound vibrations helped clear deep-seated blockages, and the advanced chakra techniques restored her energy flow. Over time, Sarah regained her vitality and emotional stability. Another case involves John, who faced persistent anxiety. By incorporating higher-frequency crystals and sacred geometry into his daily practice, he noticed a significant reduction in his anxiety levels and an increase in his overall well-being.

My own experiences have also been transformative. I recall a session where a client felt a heavy, dense energy in her heart chakra. Using a combination of sound healing and advanced chakra balancing, we cleared the blockage. The client described feeling a sense of lightness and emotional release that she hadn't experienced in years. These stories highlight the profound impact of advanced energy healing on one's life.

Advanced energy healing techniques offer a more comprehensive approach to addressing energetic imbalances. Whether using sound healing, advanced chakra techniques, or raising your vibrational frequency, these practices can bring profound healing and transformation. Incorporating these advanced techniques into your shamanic practice allows you to navigate life's challenges more efficiently and harmoniously.

6.5 WORKING WITH ANCESTORS: HEALING GENERATIONAL TRAUMA

Have you ever felt like you're carrying the weight of the world, or at least the weight of your family tree, on your shoulders? Welcome to the concept of generational trauma, where the emotional and psychological wounds of your ancestors ripple through time and land squarely in your lap. In shamanic practice, working with ancestors is not just a nod to family roots but a potent avenue for healing. Honoring and connecting with ancestors acknowledge the unbroken chain of life and wisdom passed down through generations. It's like calling a family meeting, but with spirits, to address unresolved issues and seek guidance.

Setting up an ancestor altar is a great start to connect with ancestral spirits. Choose a quiet spot in your home and place photos of your ancestors and items that remind you of them—like a piece of jewelry or a favorite book. Add candles, flowers, and any other objects that feel significant. This altar becomes a focal point for your rituals and prayers, a sacred space where you can commune with those who came before you. Rituals for invoking and communicating with ancestors can be as simple or elaborate as you wish. Light a candle, sit quietly, and speak to your ancestors. Share your thoughts, seek their wisdom, and listen for any messages. Dreamwork is another powerful method for connecting with ancestral wisdom. Before going to sleep, set the intention to meet your ancestors in your dreams. Keep a journal by your bed to record any insights or messages you receive upon waking.

Identifying and healing generational trauma involves diving deep into the family archives, but instead of dusty books, you're exploring spiritual records. Shamanic journeys can uncover ancestral wounds, revealing patterns of trauma that have been passed down through generations. During these journeys, you might encounter an ancestor who experienced significant trauma, and by witnessing their story, you can start the healing process. Rituals for releasing and healing generational trauma can involve symbolic acts like writing a letter to an ancestor, expressing forgiveness or understanding, and burning the letter to release the energy. Working with spirit guides for ancestral healing adds another layer of support. These guides can offer insights and assistance, helping you navigate the complexities of generational trauma and find pathways to healing.

Integrating the wisdom and healing received from ancestors into daily life is where the rubber meets the road. Practical steps for honoring ancestral teachings can range from incorporating tradi-tional practices into daily routines to sharing family stories with younger generations. This keeps the wisdom alive and relevant. Incorporating ancestral wisdom into your shamanic practice can deepen your connection to your roots and enhance your spiritual work. You might include specific rituals or symbols that honor your ancestors, creating a richer, more layered practice. Sharing ancestral stories and rituals with family and community honors your ancestors and fosters a sense of continuity and connection. It's like weaving a tapestry that includes threads from the past, present, and future, creating a holistic and interconnected view of life.

Ancestral Healing Exercise: Creating an Ancestor Altar

1. **Choose a Location:**
   - Find a quiet, private spot in your home.
2. **Gather Items:**
   - Photos of ancestors, personal mementos, candles, and flowers.
3. **Set Up the Altar:**
   - Arrange the items in a way that feels meaningful.
4. **Invoke Your Ancestors:**
   - Light a candle, sit quietly, and speak to your ancestors. Share your thoughts and seek their wisdom.
5. **Record Insights:**
   - Keep a journal to document any messages or insights you receive.

Setting up an ancestor altar creates a sacred space for connecting with your ancestors, honoring their legacy, and seeking their wisdom. This practice can open doors to profound healing and understanding, bridging the gap between past and present and enriching your shamanic journey.

6.6 SHAMANIC JOURNEYS TO THE UPPER AND LOWER WORLDS

Imagine having the ability to explore realms beyond our physical reality, places teeming with wisdom and healing energies. Welcome to the shamanic journeys to the Upper and Lower Worlds, a cornerstone of shamanic practice. These realms offer unique experiences and insights that can profoundly impact your spiritual growth. The Upper World is a realm of higher spiritual beings and wisdom. Think of it as a celestial library where enlightened beings reside, offering guidance and profound insights. On the other hand, the Lower World is a place of healing energies and power animals. It's like diving into an ocean of ancient wisdom, where every creature and element holds secrets of the Earth.

Preparing for these advanced shamanic journeys requires more than just setting aside time. Start by setting clear intentions for your journey. What are you seeking? Whether it's healing, guidance, or insight, clarity of purpose will guide your experience. Creating a sacred and protected space is equally important. Find a quiet, undisturbed area and cleanse it with sage or other purifying herbs. This prepares the physical space and sets the energetic tone for your journey. Techniques for entering a deeper trance state will help you access these realms more effectively. Rhythmic drumming, rattling, or even deep meditation can alter your consciousness, making navigating the spiritual world easier.

Journeying to the Upper World involves visualization techniques that help you ascend. Imagine yourself climbing a staircase, flying with the help of a spirit bird, or rising through clouds. As you ascend, focus on meeting higher spiritual beings. These entities often appear as wise elders, luminous figures, or even celestial animals. Communicate with them openly, asking for guidance and wisdom. They may answer your questions, show you visions, or impart teachings that resonate deeply with your soul. The key is to remain open and receptive, trusting the process and the beings you encounter.

Descending to the Lower World requires a different set of visualization techniques. Picture yourself entering a cave, descending a spiral staircase, or diving into water. You will encounter power animals, and spirit guides unique to this realm as you go deeper. These beings offer healing energies and ancient wisdom. Interact with them respectfully, asking for their assistance and guidance. Techniques for healing and retrieving wisdom in the Lower World often involve symbolic acts. For instance, you might envision a power animal guiding you to a healing pool or a wise elder showing you a hidden cave filled with ancient scrolls. These symbols carry deep meanings that can be integrated into your daily life.

One of the beautiful aspects of these journeys is that they are fluid and dynamic. No two experiences are the same, and the realms you explore will reveal different aspects of your spiritual path each time. The Upper World might show you a new perspective on a problem you're facing, while the Lower World could offer healing for an old wound you didn't even know you had. The richness of these experiences lies in their ability to touch different facets of your being, offering holistic healing and growth.

As you become more adept at journeying, you'll find that the insights and healing you receive become more profound and integrated into your life. The Upper World may offer guidance that helps you make pivotal decisions, while the Lower World provides the healing energy to support those changes. The balance between these realms enriches your shamanic practice, making it a profoundly transformative experience. Regularly journeying to these realms creates a continuous dialogue with the spiritual world, enhancing your understanding and connection to the universe.

CHAPTER 7

COMMUNITY AND SHARED PRACTICES

L et's start with a little story. Picture yourself at Ash Cave in Hocking Hills, Ohio, a beautiful, large overhang cave deep in the woods, where the air is filled with the rhythmic beats of drums and the scent of burning sage. Laughter and singing echo through the day as people gather in a large community circle. This isn't just a festive gathering; it's a shamanic community coming together to celebrate, heal, and connect. The sense of unity and shared purpose is palpable. This scene captures the essence of community in shamanic practice, highlighting its significance and the profound impact it can have on individual and collective well-being.

7.1 THE ROLE OF COMMUNITY IN SHAMANISM

Community in shamanism is more than just a group of people practicing together; it's a dynamic network that supports, amplifies, and enriches each individual's spiritual journey. The collective energy generated in a community setting can magnify personal experiences, making them more profound and transformative. When you engage in rituals or ceremonies within a community, the combined intentions and energies create a powerful force that can facilitate more profound healing and insights. Think of it as a spiritual potluck where everyone brings a dish, and the collective feast nourishes each person more than their individual contributions ever could.

Historically, shamanic communities have played crucial roles in their societies' social and spiritual fabric. In ancient tribes, shamans were the heart of the community, serving as healers, guides, and mediators between the physical and spiritual realms. Tribal gatherings and communal ceremonies were integral to maintaining harmony and balance within the group. These events were social gatherings and essential spiritual practices reinforcing the community's connection to the natural and spiritual worlds. The shaman's role extended beyond individual healing sessions; they were responsible for the well-being of the entire tribe, often leading rituals to ensure successful hunts, bountiful harvests, and protection from harm.

The benefits of practicing shamanism within a community are manifold. Shared rituals and ceremonies can enhance the healing process, as the collective energy amplifies the effects of the individual practices. When you participate in a communal healing ceremony, for example, the support and energy of the group can facilitate deeper emotional and spiritual healing than you might achieve alone. Furthermore, engaging in shamanic practices with others provides opportunities for learning and mentorship. Experienced practitioners can offer guidance, share wisdom, and teach techniques that can enrich your practice. This mentorship can be invaluable, especially for beginners who may feel uncertain or overwhelmed.

Emotional and spiritual support networks are another significant advantage of being part of a shamanic community. Life can be challenging, and having a group of like-minded individuals who understand and share your spiritual path can provide comfort and strength. These networks offer a safe space for sharing experiences, seeking advice, and finding solace during difficult times. Whether you're celebrating a personal breakthrough or navigating a challenging period, the support of a shamanic community can make a world of difference.

So, how do you find or create a shamanic community? Start by attending workshops and retreats. These events are excellent opportunities to meet others who share your interests and passions. Look for local shamanic practitioners or organizations that offer regular gatherings, workshops, or classes. Many communities have established groups that meet for drumming circles, journeying sessions, or seasonal celebrations. Joining these groups can provide a structured and supportive environment for your practice.

Creating a local meetup or study group is another effective way to build a shamanic community. You don't need to be an expert to start; a genuine interest and willingness to learn together are all you need. Reach out to friends, family, or colleagues who might be interested, and set up regular meetings to explore different aspects of shamanism. You can study books, watch videos, practice techniques, and share your experiences. This collaborative approach fosters community and provides a supportive network for everyone involved.

In summary, community plays a vital role in shamanic practice. It amplifies individual experiences, provides support and mentorship, and creates a powerful collective energy that enhances healing and growth. Whether you join an existing group or create your own, engaging with a shamanic community can enrich your spiritual journey and provide the support and connection you need to thrive. So, don't hesitate to reach out, connect, and become part of a vibrant shamanic community.

7.2 DRUMMING CIRCLES: CREATING COMMUNAL SACRED SPACE

Imagine a group gathered in a circle, each holding a drum. The beats start slow and steady, then grow louder and more synchronized. This isn't just a musical jam session. It's a drumming circle, a powerful communal ritual in shamanic practice. Drumming circles serve as a sacred space where individuals can connect deeply with themselves, each other, and the spiritual realm. The collective drumming creates a rhythmic bridge that facilitates trance states, making accessing spiritual insights and healing energies easier. The communal aspect amplifies the experience, allowing participants to tap into a shared energy that can be profoundly transformative.

Organizing a drumming circle might seem daunting, but it's simpler. Start by choosing a location that feels sacred and serene. This could be a quiet park corner, a spacious living room, or a community center. For years, we held drum circles at Garcia's restaurant, my family's place of business. The key is to find a place where participants can relax and focus without distractions. Next, invite participants who share an interest in shamanic practices. You don't need a large group; even a small circle of dedicated individuals can create a powerful experience. Set clear intentions for the circle. Whether it's for healing, guidance, or simply connecting with the rhythms of nature, having a focused purpose enhances the effectiveness of the ritual. Creating a sacred space involves more than just physical arrangements. Use smudging, candles, or crystals to cleanse and energize the area, making it conducive for spiritual work.

Participating in a drumming circle offers numerous benefits. The rhythmic drumming helps you connect with the natural world, mirroring the heartbeat of the Earth. This connection can ground you, making you feel more centered and balanced. Drumming circles also strengthen bonds within the community. The shared experience fosters a sense of unity and mutual support, enriching your relationships with fellow practitioners.

Additionally, these gatherings provide opportunities for collective healing and trance work. The combined energy can facilitate deeper healing and more profound spiritual experiences than you might achieve alone. Imagine the collective power of a group drumming together, each beat resonating with the others, creating a symphony of healing vibrations.

Let me share a few personal stories to illustrate the transformative power of drumming circles. A friend of mine, Sarah, was going through a tough time. She felt disconnected and overwhelmed. I invited her to join a drumming circle I was leading. Initially hesitant, she decided to give it a try. As the drumming began, she closed her eyes and let the rhythms wash over her. By the end of the session, she felt a sense of peace and connection she hadn't experienced in months. Another participant, Bob, shared how the collective energy of the circle helped him enter a deep trance state, enabling him to gain valuable insights into a personal issue he had been struggling with. These experiences are not unique. After participating in a drumming circle, many participants feel rejuvenated, inspired, and more connected to their spiritual path.

Here are a few tips if you're considering starting your drumming circle. Begin by attending existing circles to get a feel for their conduct. The Condor Eagle Society for Shamanic Studies emphasizes the importance of circle work in building a shamanic community. They suggest welcoming the opportunity to sit in a circle, recognizing shared intentions, and respecting others' perspectives. Once you're ready, gather a few like-minded individuals and find a suitable location. Set clear intentions for the circle and create a sacred space using smudging or other cleansing rituals. Start with simple rhythms and gradually build complexity as participants become more comfortable. Encourage open communication and respect within the group, ensuring everyone feels safe and supported.

Drumming circles are powerful ways to create communal sacred space, facilitating deep connections, healing, and spiritual growth. Whether you are a seasoned practitioner or a curious beginner, joining or organizing a drumming circle can enrich your shamanic practice and provide a supportive network of like-minded individuals. So, grab a drum, find a few friends, and let the rhythms guide you into a world of spiritual connection and transformation.

7.3 SHARED CEREMONIES: ENHANCING GROUP ENERGY

Imagine yourself laying on the ground with the top of your head in alignment with a mother drum in a circle with others, each person preparing for the drum journey. This isn't just any gathering; it's a shared ceremony—a powerful communal ritual that amplifies spiritual energy and self-healing. Shared ceremonies are central to shamanic practice because they harness the power of collective intention. The energy generated can be transformative when a group comes together with a unified purpose. It's like combining individual streams to form a mighty river, enhancing each participant's experience through the synergistic flow of group energy.

Planning and conducting a shared ceremony require thoughtful preparation. Start by setting a clear purpose and intention for the ceremony. A focused goal is crucial for healing, guidance, or celebrating a seasonal event. Assign roles and responsibilities to participants. This ensures that everyone has a part to play and fosters a sense of ownership and involvement.

Incorporate traditional elements and symbols to enhance the

sacredness of the ritual. This could include smudging with sage, using crystals, or creating an altar with meaningful objects. Each element should align with the ceremony's intention, creating a cohesive and powerful experience.

Shared ceremonies come in various forms, each serving a unique purpose. Seasonal celebrations, such as those marking solstices and equinoxes, honor the natural cycles and connect participants to the rhythms of the Earth. These ceremonies often involve rituals that celebrate growth, renewal, and transformation. Healing circles and group journeys are another type of shared ceremony. In these gatherings, participants come together to support one another in their healing processes. The collective energy can facilitate profound emotional and spiritual healing, offering a safe space for individuals to release old wounds and embrace new beginnings. Community blessings and initiations are also significant shared ceremonies. These rituals often mark critical life transitions, such as births, marriages, or welcoming new members into the community. They strengthen communal bonds and reinforce the group's shared values and intentions.

Consider the example of a seasonal celebration held by a shamanic community in the Midwest. The group gathers at the sacred Ash Cave to celebrate the Spring and Autumn Equinox. Each participant brought a small offering, such as a flower, a stone, or a fruit, symbolizing new growth and abundance. They created a beautiful altar with these offerings and performed various rituals, including drumming, chanting, and guided meditation to connect with the Earth's energies. The ceremony concluded with a communal feast, where participants shared food and stories, deepening their connections with one another and the natural world. This shared ceremony honored the changing season and fostered a sense of unity and renewal within the community.

Another example comes from a healing circle organized by a group of shamanic practitioners in New Mexico. The ceremony was designed to support a member undergoing a significant life transition. Each participant took turns offering words of encouragement and support, creating a powerful energy of love and healing. The group then performed a guided journey, during which they envisioned the person surrounded by healing light and supported by their spirit guides. The collective energy generated during the ceremony facilitated a profound emotional release and gave the individual the strength and clarity to navigate their transition.

Insights from diverse shamanic traditions further illustrate the power of shared ceremonies. In indigenous Siberian cultures, communal rituals often involve drumming, dancing, and using sacred plants to induce trance states and facilitate communication with the spirit world. These ceremonies strengthen communal bonds and ensure the well-being of the entire tribe. In Native American traditions, ceremonies such as the Sun Dance or the Sweat Lodge are communal rituals that promote healing, spiritual growth, and a deep connection with the Earth and the ancestors. These practices highlight the importance of community in shamanic work and the transformative power of shared ceremonies.

Shared ceremonies are a cornerstone of shamanic practice. They amplify spiritual energy, enhance individual experiences, and foster community. Whether you're celebrating the changing seasons, supporting one another in healing, or marking critical life transitions, these communal rituals create a sacred space where profound transformation can occur. So, gather your community, set your intentions, and embrace the power of shared ceremonies.

7.4 TEACHING AND SHARING SHAMANIC PRACTICES

Teaching shamanic practices is a cornerstone for preserving and continuing these ancient traditions. When knowledge is passed on, it ensures that the ancestors' wisdom doesn't fade into obscurity but remains vibrant and alive. Imagine a world where the profound insights of shamanism are lost because no one took the time to teach the next generation. Sharing knowledge helps build a knowledgeable and empowered community. It allows individuals to grow and develop their spiritual abilities, ensuring the practices evolve while remaining rooted in their authentic origins. Passing on this wisdom is like planting seeds in a garden; each seed has the potential to grow into a strong, flourishing tree, contributing to the overall health and beauty of the garden.

Creating a structured curriculum is the first step in effective teaching. This doesn't mean rigid lesson plans but rather a clear outline of what you aim to teach and the key concepts to cover. Start with the basics, such as understanding the shamanic worldview, and gradually introduce more complex practices like journeying, energy work, and healing ceremonies. Using experiential learning methods is crucial in shamanism. Hands-on experiences like guided meditations, drumming sessions, and rituals allow students to internalize the teachings and develop their skills. There needs to be more than just reading about shamanic practices; one must experience them to understand their power truly. Ensuring cultural respect and authenticity is also vital. This means teaching practices in their traditional context, acknowledging their origins, and emphasizing the importance of respecting the cultures from which they come.

Different teaching methods can be employed to share shamanic knowledge effectively. Workshops and seminars provide a structured environment where participants can immerse themselves in learning over a few days or weeks. These intensive sessions can be incredibly transformative, offering a deep dive into specific aspects of shamanism. One-on-one mentorship is another powerful method. It provides personalized guidance and support, helping students navigate their paths and address their unique challenges. This approach fosters a deep connection between teacher and student, creating a supportive and nurturing learning environment. Online courses and virtual gatherings have become increasingly popular and accessible. They offer flexibility and reach, allowing individuals worldwide to learn and connect. Virtual circles, webinars, and online workshops can bring diverse perspectives and experiences, enriching learning.

Personal stories and testimonials highlight the impact of teaching and mentorship. I remember conducting a workshop where a participant, Emma, was initially skeptical about shamanic practices. By the end of the weekend, she had connected with her spirit guide and experienced a profound sense of healing. Her testimonial spoke volumes about the transformative power of teaching. Another student, Mark, shared how one-on-one mentorship helped him overcome significant personal challenges. Through regular sessions, he learned to navigate his shamanic journeys and apply the insights he gained to his daily life. Our mentor-mentee relationship helped him grow spiritually and fostered a deep bond of trust and mutual respect.

Teaching shamanic practices is not just about imparting knowledge; it's about creating a space where individuals can explore, grow, and connect with their spiritual selves. It's about ensuring that the ancient wisdom of shamanism continues to thrive and evolve, enriching the lives of those who embrace its teachings. Teaching is a sacred responsibility that requires dedication, respect, and a genuine desire to see others succeed on their spiritual paths. Whether through workshops, mentorship, or online courses, the goal remains: to share the timeless wisdom of shamanism and empower others to carry it forward.

7.5 BUILDING A SUPPORTIVE SHAMANIC COMMUNITY

Imagine trying to navigate the spiritual path alone, without a supportive community. It's like walking through a dense forest without a map or compass. A nurturing and supportive environment is crucial for shamanic practitioners, offering emotional and spiritual support that can make all the difference in your journey. When life throws curveballs, having a group of like-minded individuals who understand your path can provide solace and strength. These communities offer opportunities for growth and collaboration, allowing you to learn from others, share experiences, and expand your understanding of shamanic practices.

Creating a supportive shamanic community starts with encouraging open communication and respect among members. Everyone should feel safe to express their thoughts and experiences without fear of judgment. Regular gatherings and check-ins are also essential. These don't have to be elaborate events; even simple, consistent meetups can foster a sense of belonging and continuity. Whether it's a weekly drumming circle, a monthly potluck, or seasonal ceremonies, these gatherings keep the community connected and engaged. Creating safe spaces for sharing and healing is another critical aspect. Designate areas where people can openly discuss their spiritual experiences, seek advice, and receive emotional support. These spaces should be free from distractions and imbued with a sense of sacredness to facilitate deep, meaningful interactions.

Community leaders are pivotal in fostering a positive and inclusive shamanic group. Influential leaders guide with integrity and compassion, setting a tone of respect and openness. They facilitate group rituals and ceremonies, ensuring everyone feels included and valued. Leaders should also be approachable and willing to listen, providing guidance and support when needed. Their primary responsibility is to create an environment where everyone feels safe, respected, and encouraged to grow spiritually. This involves leading by example and being flexible and adaptable to the community's evolving needs.

Consider the example of a thriving shamanic community in the Midwest. This group started small, with just a handful of people meeting for monthly drumming circles. Over time, they grew into a vibrant community, hosting workshops, retreats, and seasonal ceremonies. One of the keys to their success was the leadership's commitment to inclusivity and respect. They encouraged open communication, organized regular gatherings, and created safe spaces for sharing and healing. Testimonials from community members highlight the profound impact this supportive environment had on their spiritual growth and emotional well-being. One member shared how the community helped her navigate a challenging period, providing her the support and guidance to move forward with renewed strength and clarity.

Another example comes from a shamanic group in Missouri. This community focused on collaborative growth, encouraging members to share their unique skills and knowledge. They organized regular workshops where individuals could teach different aspects of shamanic practice, from journeying techniques to herbal medicine. Once a year, they hold a Great Council to bring all the members together collaboratively, enrich the group's collective knowledge, and empower individuals to participate actively in their spiritual development. The leaders of this community emphasized the importance of mutual respect and open communication, creating a nurturing environment where everyone felt valued and supported.

A supportive shamanic community can be a powerful catalyst for personal and collective transformation. By fostering open communication, organizing regular gatherings, and creating safe spaces for sharing and healing, you can build a positive and inclusive group that nurtures spiritual growth. Effective leaders play a crucial role in this process, guiding with integrity and compassion to create an environment where everyone feels respected and encouraged to explore their spiritual path. Whether you're part of an established community or looking to start your own, these principles can help you create a nurturing and supportive shamanic group that enriches the lives of all its members.

7.6 ETHICAL LEADERSHIP IN SHAMANIC PRACTICE

Imagine you're leading a group of shamanic practitioners, guiding them through rituals and ceremonies. It's not just about knowing the techniques; it's about embodying ethical leadership that sets a positive example for others. Ethical and moral considerations are crucial in shamanic communities because they ensure the integrity of the practices and protect the well-being of all participants. When you lead with ethics, you create a safe and respectful environment where everyone feels valued and supported. This fosters trust and encourages individuals to explore their spiritual paths with confidence.

As a leader, upholding ethical standards in teaching and healing is paramount. This means being transparent about your qualifications and ensuring you only teach what you have mastered. It also involves obtaining informed consent from participants before healing, clearly explaining what the process entails and what they can expect. Creating a culture of respect and inclusivity is equally essential. Encourage open dialogue, where everyone's voice is heard and respected. This enriches the community and ensures that diverse perspectives are acknowledged and valued. Addressing conflicts and challenges with integrity is another key aspect of ethical leadership. Conflicts are inevitable, but how you handle them can make or break the community. You can approach disputes with an open mind, listen to all parties involved, and strive to find a solution that honors everyone's dignity and well-being.

An effective shamanic leader's qualities are more than being knowledgeable or experienced. Compassion, humility, and authenticity are foundational traits that inspire trust and respect. A compassionate leader understands their community's emotional and spiritual needs and offers support with empathy and kindness. Humility keeps you grounded, reminding you that leadership is not about wielding power but serving others. Authenticity ensures that your actions align with your words, fostering a sense of trust and integrity. Strong communication and organizational skills are also essential. Clear communication helps you convey complex shamanic concepts easily, while organizational skills ensure that rituals, ceremonies, and gatherings run smoothly and effectively.

Let me share a story about a respected shamanic leader named Maria. Maria led a thriving community in the Southwest, known for her compassionate and inclusive approach. One of her community members, Jason, once shared how Maria's leadership had a transformative impact on his life. Jason had been struggling with deep emotional wounds and sought guidance from Maria. Jason found healing and renewed purpose through her compassionate support and ethical practices. Maria's authenticity and humility made her an approachable and trusted leader, fostering a supportive environment where everyone felt valued.

Another example comes from a leader named Jonathan, who faced significant challenges. Jonathan led a diverse group with varying beliefs and practices, sometimes leading to conflicts. Instead of asserting his authority, Jonathan approached these conflicts with humility and a genuine desire to understand all perspectives. He facilitated open discussions, allowing everyone to express their views and collaboratively find resolutions. This approach resolved the conflicts and strengthened the community's bonds and trust in Jonathan's leadership.

Ethical leadership in shamanic practice is about more than just guiding rituals and ceremonies. It's about creating a safe, respectful, and inclusive environment where individuals can explore their spiritual paths with confidence and support. By upholding ethical standards, fostering open communication, and embodying compassion, humility, and authenticity, you can lead your community with integrity and inspire others to follow.

In summary, ethical leadership ensures the integrity of shamanic practices and creates a safe and supportive environment for all participants. It involves upholding ethical standards, fostering respect and inclusivity, and addressing conflicts with integrity. Effective shamanic leaders embody compassion, humility, and authenticity and possess strong communication and organizational skills. These qualities inspire trust and respect, guiding their communities with wisdom and integrity. As we move forward, we will explore the transformative power of shamanism in the next chapter.

CHAPTER 8
TRANSFORMATIVE POWER OF SHAMANISM

8.1 PERSONAL TRANSFORMATION THROUGH SHAMANIC PRACTICES

Imagine standing at the edge of a serene lake, its surface reflecting the sky's vast expanse. As you toss a pebble into the water, concentric ripples spread out, altering the lake's mirror-like stillness. In many ways, shamanic practices function similarly, creating ripples of transformation that extend through various aspects of your life. Shamanism offers profound tools for personal transformation, leading to inner healing, enhanced self-awareness, and a strengthened spiritual connection.

At the heart of the shamanic transformation are inner healing and emotional balance. Shamanic practices help you confront and release old emotional wounds that may have been festering for years. Techniques like soul retrieval and energy cleansing can restore fragmented parts of your soul, bringing a sense of wholeness and peace. Imagine feeling a weight lifted off your shoulders as you let go of past traumas, making room for emotional balance and well-being.

Enhanced self-awareness and intuition are also significant outcomes of shamanic practice. As you engage in rituals and journeys, you peel back the layers of your psyche, revealing your true self. This heightened self-awareness enables you to make more informed decisions, trust your instincts, and navigate life's challenges more easily. Your intuition becomes a reliable guide, offering insights and wisdom that were previously hidden. It's like tuning into a radio station with perfect clarity, where every message resonates deeply within you.

Another transformative aspect of shamanism is a strengthened spiritual connection. By connecting with spirit guides, power animals, and the elements, you develop a profound sense of interconnectedness with the world around you. This spiritual bond fosters a deeper appreciation for life, nature, and the unseen realms. You begin to see the world with your eyes, heart, and soul, experiencing a sense of unity and purpose.

Specific shamanic techniques can facilitate these transformative changes. Deep shamanic journeys are a powerful way to embark on self-discovery. During these journeys, you enter an altered state of consciousness, guided by rhythmic drumming or rattling. In this state, you can explore the spiritual realms, seeking guidance and healing from spirit guides and power animals. These journeys often reveal hidden truths and insights that can lead to profound personal growth.

Rituals for releasing old patterns and beliefs are also essential for transformation. These rituals might involve writing down limiting beliefs on paper and burning them, symbolizing the release of what no longer serves you. Rituals create a sacred space for letting go of the old and welcoming the new, paving the way for personal evolution. It's like cleaning out a cluttered closet, making room for fresh, new experiences.

Working with power animals offers another avenue for personal growth. Power animals embody specific qualities and strengths that can help you navigate challenges and enhance your life. By connecting with your power animal, you can draw upon its wisdom and strength, incorporating these qualities into your daily life. Imagine having a loyal companion, offering guidance and support whenever needed.

The stages of transformation through shamanic practices often follow a predictable pattern. The initial awakening and curiosity phase is marked by excitement and wonder as you begin to explore shamanism. This stage is usually filled with new experiences and insights, sparking a more profound interest in the practice. As you continue, you enter the deepening practice and facing challenges phase. Here, you may encounter obstacles and difficulties that test your commitment. However, these challenges are growth opportunities, pushing you to delve deeper into your practice.

The final stage, integration and living the teachings, involves incorporating the wisdom and insights from shamanic practices into your daily life. This stage is about embodying the principles of shamanism, allowing them to guide your actions and decisions. You become a living testament to the transformative power of shamanism, radiating peace, wisdom, and balance.

Real-life examples and testimonials highlight the profound impact of shamanic transformation. Take Sarah, for instance, who struggled with chronic anxiety and self-doubt. She connected with a wise owl as her power animal through regular shamanic journeys and rituals. This connection helped her gain clarity and confidence, transforming her life in ways she never imagined. Or consider Joe, who felt lost and purposeless. After participating in a soul retrieval ceremony, he reclaimed fragmented parts of his soul, leading to a newfound sense of purpose and direction.

These stories illustrate the transformative power of shamanism. By engaging in shamanic practices, you, too, can experience profound changes, leading to inner healing, enhanced self-awareness, and a deep spiritual connection. The transformation journey through shamanism is a path of discovery, growth, and profound personal evolution. So, take a deep breath, open your heart, and let the ripples of transformation begin.

8.2 CASE STUDIES OF SHAMANIC HEALING SUCCESSES

Imagine a woman named Jane, plagued by chronic back pain that had been her unwelcome companion for years. Traditional medicine offered little relief, and she was desperate for a solution. Jane turned to shamanic healing, hoping for a miracle. During a session, the shaman used energy work to identify and release blockages in her energy field. Jane felt warmth and tingling as the shaman's rattles created rhythmic vibrations. Over the next few weeks, her pain diminished significantly, and she regained mobility she thought she'd lost forever. This case highlights how energy work can facilitate physical healing by addressing the underlying energetic imbalances.

Let's talk about emotional healing, a realm where shamanism truly shines. Meet Alex, a young man burdened by trauma from a tumultuous childhood. He felt disconnected and emotionally numb. During a soul retrieval session, the shaman guided Alex into a trance state, journeying to the spirit world to retrieve his lost soul fragments. Alex experienced vivid visions of his younger self, trapped in moments of fear and sadness. As these fragments were reintegrated, Alex felt an overwhelming sense of release. He cried for the first time in years, feeling lighter and more whole. The emotional release was profound, and Alex began reconnecting with his feelings, experiencing life with newfound clarity and depth.

Spiritual growth is another area where shamanism excels. Consider Jill, who felt spiritually lost and directionless. Through shamanic journeys, she sought guidance from her spirit guides. One particularly transformative session involved a journey to the Upper World, where she met a wise elder who imparted profound wisdom about her life's purpose. This experience ignited a spiritual awakening in Jill. She began to meditate regularly, seeking further guidance from her spirit guides. Over time, she discovered a passion for holistic healing and pursued a career as a Reiki practitioner. Jill's journey illustrates how shamanic practices can foster spiritual growth and clarify one's path.

Diverse examples of shamanic healing further illustrate its breadth. Take Don, who suffered from severe migraines. After multiple sessions involving energy mapping and guided journeys, his migraines subsided. Or Stephanie, who struggled with grief after losing her mother. With the help of spirit guides, she found solace and healing, feeling her mother's presence guiding her through her sorrow. Then there's Tom, who participated in a vision quest to find clarity and purpose. Spending days alone in nature, he experienced profound insights that led him to change careers and embrace a more fulfilling life.

Successful shamanic healings share common elements. Intention and trust are paramount. The practitioner and the client must approach the healing with clear intentions and trust in the process. The practitioner's skill and the client's openness create a powerful synergy. Integration is equally crucial. Healing experiences must be woven into daily life to ensure lasting change. This might involve journaling insights, creating rituals, or making lifestyle adjustments.

Consider Jenna's story. She suffered from anxiety and sought shamanic healing. After several sessions, she felt calmer and more centered. Jenna credits her transformation to the shaman's skill and her willingness to trust the process. "I was skeptical at first," she admits, "but I decided to keep an open mind. The results have been incredible." Then there's Mark, who battled depression. Shamanic healing helped him reconnect with his spirit guides, offering support and guidance. "I felt a profound shift," Mark shares. "It was like a weight lifted off my shoulders. I feel more alive and connected."

These testimonials underscore the transformative power of shamanic healing. The potential for profound change is immense, whether physical, emotional, or spiritual healing. By addressing the root causes of ailments and fostering a deep connection with the spiritual realm, shamanic practices offer a holistic approach to healing that can lead to life-changing outcomes. The stories of Jill, Alex, Mark, and others testify to the efficacy of shamanic healing, providing hope and inspiration for those seeking a path to wellness.

8.3 OVERCOMING DOUBTS AND FEARS IN SHAMANISM

Imagine you're standing at the edge of a dense forest. The path ahead is shrouded in mist, and every rustle of leaves raises the hair on the back of your neck. This is what embarking on shamanic practices can feel like for many beginners. The fear of the unknown and the spiritual realms is a common concern. It's perfectly normal to feel apprehensive about venturing into territories that are not only unfamiliar but also intangible. Interacting with spirits, journeying to other worlds, and confronting deep-seated emotions can be daunting.

Doubts about the effectiveness of shamanic techniques often linger in the minds of those new to the practice. Questions like "Will this really work for me?" or "Is this just my imagination?" are frequent. These doubts can stem from a lack of understanding or experience with spiritual practices. The skepticism isn't necessarily bad; it can keep you grounded. However, it's essential to balance skepticism with an open mind. It's like trying a new recipe—you're unsure if you'll like it, but you'll never know unless you take that first bite.

Concerns about cultural appropriation and authenticity are also valid. Shamanism has deep roots in indigenous cultures, and there's a fine line between respectful practice and appropriation. It's crucial to approach shamanic practices with respect and a willingness to learn from authentic sources. Ignorance can lead to unintentional disrespect, and it's important to be mindful of the cultural significance behind the rituals and tools you use. Imagine attending a foreign wedding—you wouldn't just crash the party without understanding the customs and traditions involved.

So, how do you overcome these doubts and fears? First, encourage open-mindedness and curiosity—approach shamanic practices with the same sense of wonder as a child exploring a new playground. Allow yourself to be curious and open to the experiences without needing immediate validation. Seek guidance from experienced practitioners who can provide insights and support. Having a mentor or a community can offer reassurance and practical advice. They've been where you are and can share their journeys, making your path less lonely and more navigable.

Taking small, manageable steps in practice can also help alleviate fears. You don't have to dive into deep shamanic journeys right away. Start with simple rituals or meditations. Gradually build your confidence and familiarity with the practices. It's like learning to swim—you wouldn't jump into the deep end without first getting comfortable in the shallow water. Each small step builds your confidence and lays the foundation for more profound, transformative experiences.

I'd like to share a few stories of individuals who overcame their initial skepticism. Take Emily, for instance. She was always a logical thinker, skeptical of anything that couldn't be quantified. However, she decided to try a simple grounding ritual, feeling a bit silly at first. Over time, she noticed a subtle but profound change in her emotional stability. "I started feeling more centered and less anxious," she said. Her initial skepticism turned into genuine belief as she experienced the benefits firsthand.

Then, David approached shamanic healing with a healthy dose of doubt. Suffering from chronic stress, he reluctantly attended a shamanic drumming circle. The rhythmic beats initially felt awkward, but soon, he found himself slipping into a meditative state. "I felt a sense of peace I hadn't experienced in years," David shared. This profound experience dispelled his doubts and opened him up to further exploring shamanic practices.

Facing and overcoming these fears can lead to deeper spiritual growth and transformation. Increased confidence and trust can enhance your openness to spiritual experiences. As you move past your doubts, you become more receptive to the wisdom and healing of shamanism. This newfound openness can enhance personal empowerment, allowing you to navigate life's challenges with greater ease and resilience. It's like finding a hidden reservoir of strength within yourself that you never knew existed.

8.4 SUSTAINING LONG-TERM SHAMANIC PRACTICE

Imagine shamanism as a plant. You can't just water it once and expect it to flourish. It requires consistent care and attention. This is why sustaining a long-term shamanic practice is crucial. Consistent practice accumulates benefits over time, such as regular exercise that strengthens your muscles. The more you engage with shamanic practices, the deeper your connection with the spiritual realms becomes. It's like tuning a radio to the right frequency; the more you practice, the more precise the signal.

Maintaining a regular practice involves setting realistic and achievable goals. You wouldn't try to run a marathon without training, so start small with your shamanic practices. Perhaps begin with ten minutes of meditation or a simple daily ritual. As you become more comfortable, gradually increase your practice time. Setting attainable goals prevents burnout and keeps you motivated. Creating a supportive environment for practice is also essential. Designate a space in your home where you can perform your rituals undisturbed. Fill it with objects that inspire you, like crystals, feathers, or candles. This space becomes your sanctuary to retreat and connect with the spiritual world.

Integrating shamanic practices into your daily routine can make them feel less like a chore and more like a natural part of your life. Consider incorporating short rituals into your morning or evening routines. Maybe you could start your day with a grounding exercise or end it with a gratitude ritual. These small practices can significantly impact over time, helping you stay connected to your spiritual path.

Of course, maintaining a long-term practice comes with its challenges. One common obstacle is managing time and energy. Life gets busy, and finding time for shamanic practices can be difficult. However, even short, five-minute rituals can be effective. The key is consistency, not duration. Another challenge is dealing with periods of doubt or stagnation. It's normal to experience these phases in any spiritual practice. When they occur, remind yourself why you started. Revisit your initial goals and the transformations you've experienced. Reflecting on your progress can reignite your motivation.

Staying inspired is another hurdle. Try exploring new techniques or rituals to keep your practice fresh and engaging. Attend workshops or read books on shamanism to expand your knowledge. Connecting with a community of like-minded individuals can also provide inspiration and support. Sometimes, hearing about others' experiences can rekindle your enthusiasm.

Long-term practitioners often have fascinating stories about their sustained practices. Take Lisa, for example. She has been practicing shamanism for over twenty years. What began as a curiosity evolved into a lifelong commitment. Over the years, she has deepened her connection with her spirit guides and developed a profound understanding of herself and the world around her. Lisa credits her regular practice with helping her navigate life's challenges with grace and resilience. She shares, "There were times when I wanted to give up, but the rewards of staying committed have been immense. My spiritual practice has become a source of strength and guidance."

Another example is Mark, who integrated shamanic practices into his daily life after experiencing a significant personal loss. Initially, he found solace in short meditations and rituals. His practice expanded to include regular shamanic journeys and energy work as he continued. Mark describes how his long-term commitment has transformed his perspective on life: "I feel more connected to everything around me. My relationships have improved, and I have a greater sense of purpose and peace."

These stories illustrate the profound benefits of sustaining a long-term shamanic practice. The cumulative effects of regular engagement with shamanic practices can lead to deep spiritual growth and transformation. By setting realistic goals, creating a supportive environment, and integrating practices into your daily routine, you can overcome challenges and stay committed to your spiritual path. The journey of long-term practice is filled with rewards, offering continuous opportunities for growth and connection.

8.5 LIVING A SHAMANIC LIFE: INTEGRATING LESSONS LEARNED

Imagine your daily routine infused with the wisdom of ancient shamanic practices. Living a shamanic life means integrating these timeless principles into every aspect of your existence, from the mundane to the profound. This approach involves applying shamanic wisdom to daily decisions and embodying respect, humility, and interconnectedness. It's not about performing rituals 24/7 but instead letting the essence of shamanism permeate your thoughts, actions, and interactions.

Applying shamanic wisdom to daily decisions can be as simple as pausing to consider the broader impact of your actions. For instance, before making a significant life choice, take a moment to meditate or consult your spirit guides. This practice can provide clarity and ensure that your decisions align with your highest good and the well-being of those around you. It's akin to having a spiritual GPS guiding you toward choices that resonate with your true self.

Embodying the values of respect, humility, and interconnectedness is another cornerstone of living a shamanic life. Respect extends to all forms of life, recognizing the spirit in every being, whether it's a towering oak tree or a tiny insect. Humility involves acknowledging that we are part of a larger whole, not the center of the universe. Interconnectedness reminds us that our actions ripple out, affecting our world. By embodying these values, you cultivate a sense of harmony and balance in your life.

Incorporating shamanic lessons into various aspects of life can be both practical and transformative. Practicing gratitude and mindfulness is a simple yet powerful way to stay connected to the present moment. Start your day by listing a few things you're grateful for, or take a mindful walk, paying attention to the sights, sounds, and smells around you. These practices ground you, fostering a deep sense of appreciation and presence.

Using rituals to mark significant life events can add a layer of sacredness to your experiences. Whether it's a birthday, a new job, or even a challenging transition, creating a ritual can help you honor and navigate these moments. Light a candle, pray, or perform a simple ceremony to celebrate or seek guidance. These rituals serve as touchstones, reminding you of your connection to the spiritual world.

Incorporating nature's connection into daily routines is another way to live a shamanic life. Spend time outdoors, even just a few minutes, in your garden or a nearby park. Engage with nature through gardening, hiking, or sitting under a tree and bare feet to the soil. These interactions help you attune to the natural world's rhythms, fostering a more profound sense of belonging and peace.

Consider the stories of individuals who have successfully integrated shamanic practices into their lives. Take Jaymi, who used shamanic drumming principles to enhance his relationships. By practicing mindful listening and respecting his loved ones' perspectives, he noticed a significant improvement in his connections. His relationships became more harmonious and fulfilling, reflecting the values of interconnectedness and respect.

Then there's Hayden, who found increased personal and professional fulfillment through shamanic practices. By incorporating daily gratitude rituals and seeking guidance from his spirit guides, he clarified his career path. This led him to pursue a profession aligned with his passions and values, resulting in greater satisfaction and success. Hayden's story illustrates how a shamanic life can lead to a more meaningful and balanced existence.

Embracing shamanic principles can lead to a greater sense of purpose and direction. When your actions and decisions align with your spiritual values, you experience a deeper understanding of fulfillment and clarity. This alignment fosters enhanced emotional and spiritual well-being as you feel more connected to your true self and the world around you.

Living a shamanic life also strengthens your connection with the natural world. By spending time in nature and recognizing the spirit in all living beings, you cultivate a sense of unity and harmony with the environment. This connection nurtures a profound appreciation for the beauty and wisdom of the natural world, enriching your life in countless ways.

8.6 EMPOWERING OTHERS THROUGH YOUR SHAMANIC JOURNEY

Imagine standing in a circle of people, each sharing their spiritual experiences. The air is charged with a sense of unity and understanding. This is the power of sharing one's shamanic journey. When you share your experiences, you inspire and guide others on their spiritual paths. Your stories can spark curiosity, offer insights, and comfort those just starting their journey. It's like lighting a candle in a dark room; your light helps others find their way.

Sharing your journey also helps build a supportive and empowered community. When individuals come together to share their experiences, they create a mutual support and encouragement network. This community becomes a safe space where everyone can explore their spirituality without judgment. It's a place where people can learn from each other's successes and challenges, fostering a sense of belonging and collective growth. Imagine being part of a group where everyone is committed to personal and spiritual development. The energy and support from such a community can be transformative.

So, how can you empower others? Start by leading through example and sharing your personal stories. Be open about your experiences, both the highs and the lows. Your honesty and vulnerability can make others feel comfortable sharing their own stories. Offer guidance and mentorship to those who are new to shamanic practices. Share the techniques and rituals that have worked for you, and be available to answer questions and provide support. Creating inclusive and respectful spaces for learning is also crucial. Ensure that everyone feels welcome and valued, regardless of their background or level of experience. This inclusivity fosters a sense of safety and encourages open exploration.

Empowering others has reciprocal benefits. As you help others on their spiritual paths, you deepen your understanding of shamanic practices. Teaching and mentoring require you to explain your knowledge clearly, which can enhance your grasp of the subject. Additionally, empowering others strengthens community bonds. When you invest in the growth of others, you create a network of support that benefits everyone, including yourself. There's also immense joy in witnessing others transform. Seeing someone overcome their fears, find their purpose, or achieve emotional healing is profoundly rewarding. It's like watching a flower bloom; your guidance and support helped nurture that growth.

Consider the story of Jody, who began her shamanic journey feeling lost and disconnected. Through the mentorship and support of a more experienced practitioner, she found her path and eventually became a mentor and started a holistic center. Jody now leads workshops and supports others, creating a ripple effect of empowerment and growth. Then there's Hayden, inspired by the stories shared in a community drumming circle. He felt encouraged to explore shamanic practices further and eventually became a respected leader in his community. Hayden's journey is a testament to the power of shared experiences and mutual support.

These stories highlight the transformative impact of empowering others. When you share your journey and support others, you contribute to a cycle of growth and transformation. This exchange of wisdom and support creates a thriving community where everyone can flourish. Empowering others not only enriches their lives but also deepens their spiritual practice. It's a beautiful cycle of giving and receiving, where everyone benefits.

As we move forward, remember that your journey is not just yours. It has the power to inspire, guide, and support others. By sharing your experiences and offering your wisdom, you contribute to a collective journey of growth and transformation. Your light can help others find their way, creating a more connected and empowered community. So, keep sharing, supporting, and watching as your journey enriches the lives of those around you.

KEEPING THE JOURNEY ALIVE

Now that you've completed *The Shaman's Path for Beginners*, you have all the tools to begin your journey toward healing and balance. The knowledge you've gained can guide you in your personal growth and self-discovery.

But before you move forward, I'd like to ask for your help passing that knowledge on.

By leaving your honest review on Amazon, you can show other curious souls where they can find the guidance they're seeking. You'll help keep the spirit of shamanism alive by inspiring others to explore this path.

Thank you for your support. Shamanism thrives when we share our experiences—and you're helping me do just that.

Scan the QR code to leave a review.

—Iggy Garcia

CONCLUSION

Well, here we are, dear reader. We've trekked through the dense jungles of shamanic knowledge, navigated the winding paths of ancient wisdom, and paused to reflect on the still waters of spiritual insight. It's been quite the journey. And don't worry; there were no altitude-induced tree conversations this time—just pure, grounded exploration of shamanism.

Let's take a moment to recap what we've covered. We started our journey with the foundations of shamanism, understanding its interconnected worldview where every leaf, rock, and breeze holds a spirit. We delved into the roles of shamans in ancient cultures and their responsibilities as healers, guides, and spiritual mediators. We met spirit guides and power animals, those mystical allies ready to offer us wisdom and protection.

From there, we moved on to practical techniques. We learned how to journey into the spiritual realms, connect with our spirit guides, discover our power animals, and use drumming to enter trance states. We even explored how to set up a sacred space because, let's face it, everyone needs a little sanctuary from the chaos of modern life.

In the healing chapters, we explored soul retrieval, energy work, drumming, and the healing power of nature's elements. We sipped on the wisdom of sacred plants and danced to the rhythms of healing drums and rattles. We understood the importance of ceremonies and rituals in fostering profound transformation and maintaining spiritual balance.

We also touched on the cultural context and authenticity of shamanic practices. Furthermore, we examined the rich tapestry of Siberian, Amazonian, Andean, and North American traditions, stressing the importance of respect and ethical practice. Avoiding cultural appropriation and honoring the roots of shamanism became our guiding principles as we applied the knowledge to our urban, suburban, and rural lives.

We then brought shamanism into our daily lives, integrating simple rituals, connecting with nature, and using shamanic techniques for stress relief and personal growth. Whether sipping coffee with a touch of spiritual mindfulness or taking a purposeful nature walk, we found ways to weave shamanism into the fabric of our everyday existence.

Finally, we explored the transformative power of shamanism, highlighting personal growth, emotional healing, and spiritual connection. We shared in the community's strength, the importance of shared practices, and the ethical leadership that sustains these traditions.

Now, what's the takeaway? Shamanism, at its core, is about connection. It's about feeling the earth's pulse beneath your feet, listening to the whispers of the wind, and recognizing the spirit in all things. It's about healing—not just physical ailments but emotional and spiritual wounds. It's about growth, discovering your true self, and navigating life's challenges with wisdom and grace.

So, what now? Here's your call to action. Don't let this book gather dust on a shelf. Take what you've learned and put it into practice. Start small—maybe with a morning gratitude ritual or an evening meditation. Go on a shamanic journey, connect with your spirit guides, or discover your power animal. Set up a sacred space in your home, somewhere you can retreat for peace and reflection.

Engage with nature. Take a mindful walk in the park, sit by a river, or gaze at the stars. Participate in community drumming circles or shared ceremonies. Seek workshops or retreats to deepen your understanding and connect with like-minded individuals. Honor the traditions, respect the practices, and always approach with an open heart and mind.

Remember, you don't have to do it all at once. Shamanism is a lifelong journey, not a race. Take your time, explore, and grow at your own pace. Trust the process and be patient with yourself. You've got this.

In the words of a wise shaman, *"We are but a speck on the timeline of life, but a powerful speck we are!" –Iggy Garcia.* Wherever you are on your path, know you are precisely where you need to be. Embrace the journey with curiosity and courage. Let the rhythms of the drum guide you, the whispers of the wind inspire you, and the wisdom of the earth ground you.

Thank you for walking this path with me. May your journey be filled with profound insights, deep healing, and endless wonder. And remember, it's not about the destination. It's about the journey. So, keep exploring, growing, and always staying connected to the spirit in all things.

Here's to your continued journey on the shamanic path. Be well, be curious, and remember —IT'S GOOD TO BE HERE!

Warmest blessings,

Iggy

REFERENCES

Eight Core Beliefs of Shamanism https://shamanicdrumming.com/core-beliefs-of-shamanism.html

The Three Shamanic Worlds - by Roel Crabbé https://www.roelcrabbe.com/the-three-shamanic-worlds/

Shamanism | Definition, History, Examples, Beliefs, Practices ... https://www.britannica.com/topic/shamanism#:

Power Animals: Connecting with Your Animal Spirit Guide https://drstevenfarmer.com/power-animals-connecting-with-your-animal-spirit-guide/

How to take a shamanic journey - Alchemessence https://www.alchemessence.com/blog/how-to-take-a-shamanic-journey-step-by-step-guide

How to Connect With Your Spirit Guide https://www.wikihow.com/Connect-With-Your-Spirit-Guide

Ultimate Guide To Spirit Animals, Power Animals & Totems https://www.spiritanimal.info/

Shamanic Drumming https://shamanicdrumming.com/

what is shamanic soul retrieval | treatments - Triyoga https://triyoga.co.uk/blog/treatments/shamanic-soul-retrieval/#:

Shamanic, Energy & Intuitive Healing Methods ∴ WholeSpirit https://www.wholespirit.com/personal-evolution-counseling-sessions-spiritual-shamanic-energy-intuitive-healing-north-carolina-nc/healing-counseling-modalities-used-in-personal-evolution-counseling/

Shamanic Healing: Finding our balance with the Five ... https://www.mysticartspiritmedicine.com/post/shamanic-healing-finding-our-balance-with-the-five-elements-in-nature

Plants, Shamans, and the Spirit World - USDA Forest Service https://www.fs.usda.gov/wildflowers/ethnobotany/Mind_and_Spirit/shamans.shtml#:

Shamanism | Definition, History, Examples, Beliefs ... https://www.britannica.com/topic/shamanism

The Ethics of Shamanic Healing https://omegahub.co.uk/shamanic-healing/ethics-of-shamanic-healing/

Shamanism: Approaching Indigenous Wisdom with Care ... https://shamaniceducation.org/shamanism-approaching-indigenous-wisdom-with-care-and-respect/

Shamanism: Approaching Indigenous Wisdom with Care ... https://shamaniceduca tion.org/shamanism-approaching-indigenous-wisdom-with-care-and-respect/

Shamanic Wisdom for Invoking the Sacred in Everyday Life https://braidedway.org/shamanic-wisdom-for-invoking-the-sacred-in-everyday-life/

How Does Shamanism Relate to Nature and Ecology? https://www.embracingshaman ism.org/2023/08/how-does-shamanism-relate-to-nature-and-ecology/#:

How Shamanism Can Help Beat Modern-Day Stress https://www.johnsonchong.com/how-shamanism-can-help-beat-modern-day-stress/#:

Unlocking Intuition and Insight with Shamanic Practices https://www.earth-intranet.com/blog/unlocking-intuition-and-insight-with-shamanic-practices

Traditional Native American Vision Quest - Medicine of One https://medicineofone.com/vision-quest/traditional-native-american-vision-quest/#:

A CORE SHAMANIC THEORY OF DREAMS https://www.shamanism.org/articles/pdfs/ShamanicTheoryDreams3-11.pdf

How to Create a Medicine Wheel: Steps, Considerations ... https://www.touched byanangelspiritualcentre.ca/how-to-create-a-medicine-wheel-steps-consider ations-and-insights/

What We Can Learn From Shamanic Healing https://www.ncbi.nlm.nih.gov/pmc/articles/PMC1447282/

Shamanic Community https://www.shamanism.dk/shamanic-community

Effective Core Shamanic Drumming Circles https://www.shamanism.org/effective-core-shamanic-drumming-circles/#:

Exploring Shamanic Rituals: Shamans in Diverse Cultures https://www.miragenews.com/exploring-shamanic-rituals-shamans-in-diverse-1261415/

Shaping the Shift: Shamanic Leadership, Memes, and ... https://link.springer.com/arti cle/10.1007/s10551-018-3900-8

The Transformative Power of Shamanic Wisdom https://shamaniceducation.org/the-transformative-power-of-shamanic-wisdom/

The Beauty and Healing of the Shamanic Experience https://enchantedcshel.medium.com/the-beauty-and-healing-of-the-shamanic-experience-11dfc4a03cfd

Doubt (Samshaya): The Third Obstacle to Spiritual Practice https://www.awakening self.com/doubt-samshaya-the-third-obstacle-to-spiritual-practice/#:

Long-term Outcomes of Shamanic Treatment for ... https://www.ncbi.nlm.nih.gov/pmc/articles/PMC3383158/

Genaro Garcia Von-Lembcke (Chaman) The Condor Eagle Society

Luzmila Lembcke Garcia (Chaman) The Condor Eagle Society

Juan Osco Dongo http://www.juanoscochaman.com

Philip Cloudpiler Landis http://www.nemenhah.org

Jonathan Wellamotkin Landis http://www.nemenhah.org
Jario Osco Dongo (Chaman) Rimac Pacha
Master Shaman Yankunta http://yankunta.wixsite.com